I truly cherish my friendship with Steve and admire his free spirit. What I love about our friendship is that it never gets old. He is a friend that I can always count on to be there through good and bad times.

Marcia Mehrtens

Steve is a trailblazer and inspiration. He's the most grounded and connected person I've ever known. You want high vibes? Get to know this guy!

Candice Suter

I met Steve when I was assigned to Scott AFB right after Basic training, 1986. Although we were in different work areas, I somehow got absorbed into Steve's ever-growing circle of friends. This meant going to a music, dance, pub every weekend. On one such occasion, I was set up on a blind date. We've been married 35 years now. Steve was there. Steve gives 100% to everything he does, family commitments, job challenges, wild adventures, and mostly his friends. For a rare few of us, we have been chosen to be Steve's forever family. We wish him success in all his future wild adventures. We love him always and forever.

Jim and Barb Dungan

It's been more than twenty-seven years since my friendship with Steve began! Steve is more than a friend...he is like my dear brother. Oh, yes, we've had our share of squabbles, as most siblings do, but those wonderful moments of undeniable connection far outnumber our silly quarrels. We wept together when we felt like there was no one else listening. Even the laughs came so naturally between us because we know each other so deeply. He is always there for me when it seems like the weight of the world is on my shoulders. And that precious love just keeps on growing. I love you, Steve, even more than yesterday.

Mary Schaefer

MY LIGHTS

The True Story of an Authentic Life

STEVE ZEIGER

My Lights
The True Story of an Authentic Life
Steve Zeiger

Published by Own Your Glow Press, Prairie du Rocher, IL

Project Management and Book Design: Davis Creative, LLC / CreativePublishingPartners.com
Editor: Cheryl Roberts Oliver
Copyeditor: Karen Tucker, CommaQueenEditing.com

Publisher's Cataloging-in-Publication
(Provided by Cassidy Cataloguing Services, Inc.).

Names: Zeiger, Steve, author.

Title: My lights : the true story of an authentic life / Steve Zeiger.

Description: Prairie du Rocher, IL : Own Your Glow Press, [2023]

Identifiers: ISBN: 979-8-9879484 0-8 (paperback) | 979-8-9879484-1-5 (ebook) | LCCN: 2023905440

Subjects: LCSH: Zeiger, Steve. | Sexual minorities--United States--Biography. | Gay military personnel-- United States--Biography. | Self-actualization (Psychology) | Individual differences. | LCGFT: Autobiographies. | BISAC: BIOGRAPHY & AUTOBIOGRAPHY / LGBTQ+. | BIOGRAPHY & AUTOBIOGRAPHY / Military. | FAMILY & RELATIONSHIPS / LGBTQ+.

Classification: LCC: HQ75.8.Z45 A3 2023 | DDC: 306.766092--dc23

To define is to limit.

— Oscar Wilde

A meaningful life is not being rich, being popular, being highly
educated or being perfect. It is about being real, being humble,
being able to share ourselves and touch the lives of others.
It is only then that we can have a full, happy, and contented life.

— Anonymous

Table of Contents

This book is dedicated to "My Lights" -
all the people who supported me through different stages
of my life, showing me it was safe to trust and giving me the
love I needed to become the man I am today.

Introduction

I didn't know this at the time, but I was creating and starting to live a transcendentalist life. Later in life, I read Henry David Thoreau and discovered I was mirroring the way he lived. I had a deliberate life, free of possessions, with a focus on my inner self and deeper meanings of what it meant to be alive. The solitude and peace I gained living alone and away from society was measured by my understanding of self and the way I approach life, uninfluenced by people and things. I have always been strong-minded and, most times, stayed true to my values. When I lost that strength or self-discipline for a time, it always came back.

My idea of a good life is to be aware of all that I do or do not allow into that life: I allow what is good for me to grow and relate to the Universe on my terms relative to my character, virtues, and humor, all of which are wrapped in love, acceptance, and integrity. For the most part, I will be alone. Fairness is paramount. I don't judge others but stay away from energies that don't fit my ideals of quality and peace. I am reflective of my entire past and have come a long way, primarily on my own. I can say without doubt that I am proud of all that I have created for myself and others. I feel good on the inside, and that's what matters to me. "Live and let live" is not just a phrase to me but a way of life. I live intentionally, bringing to fruition my own peace that I find in things that interest me and challenging myself with things that I have never tried before. I live an honest life, not just outwardly, but also inwardly. I hold myself accountable for everything I do. I am a minimalist to the core. I realize that time is valuable—more valuable than anything else. I know that when a moment is gone, it will never return. It is a commodity I don't squander. I used to freely give my time to people without even questioning it, but I am more prudent these days.

I pay attention to nature and appreciate the energy it gives to me. I value living things that bring beauty and grace to the world. I'm at peace in nature. For a while, I placed value on the wrong things, but I finally learned to value the things that bring me joy. I will never get back the time I wasted on situations created by others, worrying about opinions of people whose opinions didn't matter, or trying to create a situation so someone could be in my life who shouldn't have been there in the first place. I lived with insecurity trying to make friends with the wrong people, ignoring my instincts and beliefs. Every single time, my instincts proved right. Now I leave what doesn't feel energetically right. Fortunately, time and age have made me wiser.

When I encounter people who have toxic views of their world, I wonder to myself (and once in a while will ask them), "What have you learned about yourself up to this point in your life?" Their answers, if they bother, are very telling. I know now why my soul chose to be born into my family in October of 1962. I chose what would grow my soul and teach me to be a better, more decent person when faced with adversity. I believe I was born when and where I was to practice and teach tolerance.

Later in life, I thrived, but not until I truly realized who I was, which was generally following heartache and sadness. I was subjected to people who failed completely where tolerance and acceptance were concerned. That perception started changing as I got older and more accomplished. Most people could see who I was and respect my self-confidence. I have learned that being compassionate, kind, loving, sincere, understanding, and having integrity are not just attributes that are important to me, but more of what the world really needs. These were qualities I was born with; unfortunately, they were not looked upon as strengths where I grew up. I was expected to be like the people I was around, accepting what was important to them. Instead, I shook their foundation when I did not follow their rules, their expectations. I stood for myself, on my own. That's a strength none of them had for themselves, and I frightened them.

Being masculine for me took different forms. I was foreign to my parents and their families in the way I thought and acted. They didn't know how to react or accept such a different approach to life. All they knew was farming. They only knew how to be men and women, without any question of their sexual identity, marrying and having families. They followed a blueprint already in place, organized and laid out for them without any desire to live a different purpose, or even question what their true purpose may have been. Growing up with my family and the people I knew, I felt like it was my fault for making them embarrassed, looking bad, or bringing them shame. It took me a long time to overcome second-guessing myself on every level. I made some personal decisions that went against who I was and became accustomed to thinking I couldn't do anything right; time and again, I was told or shown that pretty much everything I did was wrong. This permeated throughout my childhood and into my high school years. It became part of me and, to this day, remains a theme with my family. However, with age and wisdom learned from accomplishments, their negative opinions of me no longer matter. I have boundaries in place that I stand firmly behind. The confidence I was born with—learning to talk, walking, being potty trained, eating solid food—evaporated as I tried to fit the expectations of my family. I think back on all this and truly wonder how I made it out alive with any life-sustaining qualities and values intact. It has taken me almost a lifetime to regain the confidence I naturally held, that each child is born with.

People I knew who were the most insecure, the ones who didn't have self-confidence, tried breaking my spirit. Who I was, how I thought, what I believed was as different from all of them as it could possibly be, and so I was made to feel unacceptable and damaged as I grew up. To this day, they still try to make me believe this, even given all the life experiences and growth I have achieved.

This is my purpose in writing this book. It has taken courage to put my life on paper, exposing myself and others, but my intention is simple. I'm not the only one who grew up feeling unacceptable and damaged. I'm not the only one who arrived on earth with a different blueprint than one that fit their family's or society's expectations. My desire is that what I have learned and am sharing will help others learn to love themselves, as each of us must. The best of us begins and ends with self-awareness, self-love, and self-respect.

1 : My Parents and Family

The beginnings of both my parents were as humble as you can imagine.

My future existence started taking shape in February 1940 with the birth of my father in a rural farming area around Fults, Illinois. Dad was the second oldest and second boy to my grandparents. Dad nearly died when he was born prematurely and developed complications with pneumonia. My grandma said he was turning blue. They were so thankful he survived, and so am I. This, along with Dad's personality, made Grandma feel closer to him.

They were farmers, so life for them was very busy and hard, to say the least. Since this was all they knew, not having anything else to compare it to, it didn't bother them. The only interests they had outside their home was with the church and things it supported. They didn't have any money except what was being produced from the farm. I remember my grandma telling the story of hanging milk and cheese down in the well to keep them cool and from spoiling because they didn't have a refrigerator. My grandparents created a home life in the 1940s like everyone of their generation and made do with what they had. At a very young age, both Dad and his older brother were expected to work the farm with my grandfather, so as the boys started growing up, their life was already formed. I don't believe either of them questioned their future, dictated by the norms of where they were being raised, of getting married and starting their own families. That was the expectation. As Dad grew into his teens, he was mischievous. He liked practical jokes, and his family got the brunt of his creativity on that. He once dropped a firecracker down the basement stairs while my grandpa was carrying a case of eggs. Grandpa's back was to my dad, so he didn't see him. As the firecracker dropped from step to step, my dad was worried as it got closer to Grandpa. When it went off, Grandpa dropped the case of eggs and the chase ensued. Grandpa chased my dad up to the barns on the bluff to catch him and give him a spanking. The way the story goes, Dad was laughing so hard he could hardly run, which made Grandpa that much more furious. When Grandpa caught up with him, he definitely got a spanking. My dad's ability to make people laugh and catch them off guard with his pranks never left him. This is where I get the pranking gene; it's an honest-born trait in me.

Before he was a teenager, my dad's sister and brother were born, and a few years later, one more son and, lastly, a baby girl, Little Mary, was born into the family. When the boys were partway through their ninth grade, Grandpa pulled them out of school so they could work full-time in the fields. This was an acceptable and necessary practice then—part of running a farm. The societal norms of that time and in that rural setting weren't questioned. Dad stayed within the confines of that for the most part, but he ventured outside the norms of what my grandparents and society had set when he could. He was curious about the outside world and wanted to know more about it. Dad and Gerald, a buddy of his, drove to a nearby town where Dad found a job for a brief time. It was in the late spring, I think, when everything was mostly done in the fields, so he could leave. He found a job in metal working and made himself a ring, which he would eventually give to my mom when they started dating. He and Gerald both worked for a bit, including a temporary painting job. I recall a photo they had taken of themselves. Since neither of them had finished high school, they didn't have graduation pictures for their families, so they had a professional picture taken of themselves. They looked quite dashing.

Dad loved cars and having his independence, but he and his brother had to share a 1952 gray Ford. On a Saturday afternoon, after his farming chores were done, he would take his car out to Prairie du Rocher and drag race on a straight half-mile stretch with his friend Gerald. I guess you could say

Dad was a bit of a motor head. He liked mechanics and working on motors. When Dad was dating age, my grandma would wash the car for him if he were in the fields so it would be clean when he went to pick up his date. It didn't matter how busy Grandma was, she made time to do this. He was a handsome man. He loved Elvis Presley and James Dean, his era's idols, and modeled himself after them. Dad had the thickest, blackest hair; when he put grease in it, it would shine beautifully, with the sheen visible in some of the black-and-white photos that we have.

When I was a kid, I used to watch him get ready, and his hair still looked like that. He did not lack in the looks department. All the girls in that area wanted to be with him, and he knew how to treat a lady. Dad had a softness to him; he had his good looks, but his heart stood out, which added to his charm. He had a soft, loving, kind, caring heart, which showed empathy and respect. Everyone loved Dad because he was approachable and easy to talk with. He was a nice guy, always looking for the good in others, and was there to help if anyone needed it, without question. He was a man of strong character and integrity. When I think of what a man is, I think of him. He was a gentle man with a strong stature. He was a fashionable guy too; there are pictures of him standing in a modeling stance in the yard and in the driveway. He definitely had a high level of self-esteem and confidence in himself; however, he never let that go to his head. He enjoyed looking nice and took good care of his things to make them last. The tractors and farm equipment got a wash and a polish every Saturday afternoon. When my siblings and I were old enough, we did it with him. I could see why so many people regarded him with such respect.

My existence was solidified with the birth of my mom in 1942 to my other set of grandparents, both of Prairie du Rocher, Illinois. Born into a farm family, her beginnings were humble as well. She was named after both of her grandmothers. Ironically, Mom was also born premature, which if you think about it was remarkable that both she and my dad survived during that era. She was supposed to have been born in June, but one day as my grandmother was washing clothes, she tripped and fell over a wash tub, which induced her labor, so Mom was born in April, and with the power of the Universe, solid-ified that I and my siblings could be born.

The third oldest, Mom had a distinct personality. She was quiet by nature and liked her solitude, away from everyone else. I remember my great uncle, her uncle, saying he would try to take her picture when he would come home on leave, but she would have nothing to do with it. Although never lonely, she liked being alone, even as a youngster. She was focused and didn't need anyone or anything to motivate her. She did it herself. Mom was deliberate in her actions; she did what she thought was right and had a friendly personality.

Her dad, my grandfather, was a good man. A veteran of WWI, he was discharged in Puget Sound, Oregon, so on his way back, he took his time and visited the areas he passed through. A wanderer and adventurer, he would stop at Indian reservations and stay with Indian tribes and make friends with them along the way. Mom has pictures of him with the Native Americans out West. When he met my grandmother, he was twenty years older than she was. They married and then honeymooned in Wyoming.

Everyone in town liked him. He drank quite a bit, but I think that was part of that generation. Along with being a traveler and an explorer, he was a good businessman; however, he kept all his money transactions in his head, not writing anything down, which would come back to haunt my grandma. He was a good father to his kids. Mom tells the story about when they needed new shoes, my grandpa would have a cow butchered for meat, then he would tan the hide and have mom and her two older siblings spread salt on the hide to dry it. He would then take it to town and have new shoes made for all of them. They were all so young when he passed that Mom had few memories of him. I like to think he was a very liberal thinker. I would have loved to have met him. He died in 1949 from a brain hemorrhage. Mom said that when he died, people in town who owed him money never paid up because there was no record of it. Instead of people doing the right thing and paying their debt to Grandma, they turned away and never did. Mom said they likely could have starved as my grandma didn't work. I can't imagine how hard it must have been. Mom was only seven years old when he passed. Three more siblings had been born and my grandma was pregnant, putting her under a lot of stress with all those kids, no money coming in, and a farm to run. Somehow she knew she would make it; she just had to figure out a way. I know my mom gets her strength to survive from her mother. As the story goes, Grandma got a job working in the laundry at the hospital in Red Bud, a town about eight miles from where they lived. Grandma saw that Mom was responsible and mature, even at that young age, so she leaned on her and trusted her with cleaning and taking care of the younger siblings. Even though there were two older siblings, Grandma saw in Mom the responsibility she knew would be required. When Mom and her sisters got into grade school, they worked in the cafeteria so they could get a free meal.

Food at home consisted of a piece of bread with cream and molasses in the center. That was the meal on many nights. Grandma had to go to work, so Mom was left to get the younger kids to school, clean the house, make meals, plus she had a part-time job after school cleaning a house for the people who owned the town store. These people were wealthy by the standards of the day. Mom would save her money by hiding it behind a drawer in a dresser. At an early age, Mom became keenly aware that if she were going to make it, she would have to be even more thrifty and creative with her money and not talk about it.

Mom was smart and strong-willed and didn't take much from anyone. She held her ground and was deliberate in what she said. One winter, a cow gave birth to a calf down in the pasture in the woods. Mom could hear it crying out for its mother. Mom walked toward the cries and found the calf. She picked it up and carried it up the hill to the barn so it wouldn't freeze and so it could suckle its mother. Her early years held hard life lessons. When she got into high school, Mom found her own way. She used to make clothes for herself and her youngest sister. She would enter fashion shows the school put on. (Another predilection of mine for modeling came from both my parents.) Mom was beginning to accept herself and what talents she had. It was around this time that Mom and Dad met. Dad was twenty years old, and she was in her senior year of high school. Voted best-looking in her class, Mom was proud of who she was. Her grades stayed high, and she excelled in all subjects. I've been told that when she graduated, she earned a thousand-dollar scholarship to attend a college. In 1960, that was a lot of money. She met Dad at Fort de Chartres, an old French fort built in the 1700s to protect the land for the French to settle in that area. After about a year of dating, he proposed. In December 1959, my dad's sister Mary was born. Her birth completed Dad's family.

When Mom and Dad had announced they would be getting married, Grandma had Mom invite Dad's side of the family over to have supper so the families could meet. Grandma asked Mom what she should make. Mom's reply was, "I don't care what you make, just make a lot of it. His family can eat." I still laugh at this when we reminisce. Another time Mom invited Dad over to eat, Grandma made boudin. Boudin is a French meal of blood-based sausage. Mom's people were primarily French; Dad's were German. Germans didn't eat this sort of thing. My grandma put that sausage on Dad's plate, and when he cut into it and saw how black it was with a bit of blood coming out, Dad turned to Mom and said, "I can't eat this." I still laugh about that when I hear it being talked about. As soon as Mom graduated in May 1960, they were married the following month. Her dream of going to college started to evaporate as she was now a wife of a budding farmer in his own right.

In 1961, the Vietnam conflict was beginning to take shape, and the drafts were beginning. Mom told me the story of how Dad's parents and her mom were on her so fiercely to get pregnant to keep dad out of being drafted. With such pressure, she felt her voice didn't matter. She finally got pregnant with me. She told me that's how I came about. I think she resented this stage in her life because she had a scholarship to go to school but couldn't use it because Dad proposed, and to further seal this, she had to get pregnant to keep Dad out of the war.

I started my journey of life in October 1962. Mom and Dad moved to the farm in Fults, which was where I would do most of my growing up. Eventually, they bought the farm and made it theirs.

I don't remember anything, as I was so young, but from the pictures I see, I was a calm baby. My eyes are focused, reading life around me, observing and processing everything. Grandma, my mother's mother, commented once that I cried a lot. Mom said, "You weren't like that." Later on in life, I surmised I probably wasn't happy being born or felt I had made a wrong decision in the realm of the souls to choose to be born. When I look back at the pictures of Mom and myself at the same age, we had the same intense expressions on our faces—no smiles, just staring at whatever was being shown to us with the same degree of emotions.

I believe my innate ability to survive was a Universe-given trait in me. Maybe I also knew the journey I chose was going to be difficult to live out. My drive to truly be myself had begun.

My parents' firstborn, I am also the eldest grandchild on my dad's side. I was born two years and ten months after my Aunt (Little) Mary. We were so close in age that to the outside community, especially when we started going to school, it was assumed she was my sister rather than an aunt. No one knew, then, that her birth would play such a vital role not just in my life, but for all her nieces and nephews. Her birth proved to be a godsend for the entire family. She could relate to me and her younger nieces and nephews and still relate to her own siblings, who were our parents and much older than she was. Her siblings watched out for her and protected her as she was the youngest in their family. I'm pretty sure the family was shocked to find out my grandparents were having another baby when the three oldest of their kids were about to be on their own with marriages and starting their own families.

When I was eighteen months old, my sister and brother were born (twins). I was moved from the bottle and diapers to solid food and potty-trained quickly. Already walking by this time, my parents accelerated my development because they didn't want to raise three kids in cloth diapers and on the bottle. Mom couldn't do that and help Dad run the farm. The normal development time I would have had as a toddler was cut short. I must have been a quick study, as I took to all of it quickly and assume this is why I've adapted to so many things throughout my life. Even at that young age, I must have realized that this needed to happen.

My cousins, Denise and Johnny, were born by this time. Denise was three months younger than me, and Johnny was eleven months younger. I was always closer to Denise and Johnny, likely because we were the oldest ones, which set us apart. The three of us were together all the time.

I have two Aunt Marys. We called my uncle's wife Big Mary because she was an adult, and Dad's baby sister Little Mary because she was a kid. That's how we distinguished between them when we talked about them.

I grew up and interacted with my younger cousins primarily when we were at Grandma's house. Mom and her sisters-in-law would always go to my dad's mother's house to kill and clean chickens, can fruits, prepare food for winter, or to quilt. So, Denise, Johnny, and I were babies together all the time. Aunt (Big) Mary, Denise's mom, tells the story that I used Denise as my teething ring, biting her until she would scream and cry. Aunt Mary caught me doing it. One day, I let out a huge scream and cry; Mom came running into the living room and found me upset and I guess in pain. Mom asked Aunt Mary what had happened, and she said, "He was biting Denise again, so I bit him. That should stop him from doing that." Apparently, it did.

On my mom's side, I was the fourth out of the first five grandkids—all boys. I was socially acclimating to them too, but not as easily as I did with Denise and Johnny. The boys were more aggressive and rougher. I was a nonaggressive, easygoing, nonconfrontational type of kid. Later I learned about and understood the characteristics of the libra, which is my zodiac sign. I didn't like aggressive people, so I shied away from them. I knew at a very early age the personalities of people I felt comfortable around and the ones I didn't. At home, living, and growing up, I could see from pictures in our family photo album of me looking over my sister and brother in a protective manner. Being the eldest, my innate sense of protection kicked in. I was walking, and my confidence was growing. I think my personality was strong even back then. When I was four, Mom and Dad dropped my siblings and me at Grandma and Grandpa's house so they could go to the hospital. My youngest brother was born, who then completed my family. I remember Mom and Dad bringing him home from the hospital and laying him on the couch to change his diaper. I saw what I thought was a pecan shell on his belly. I started to grab it. Mom pulled my hand away and said, "Don't touch that. It's a sore and it's healing." I realized much later that that was his umbilical cord rotting off.

2 : Lights in My Meadow

I began to be aware of and understand feelings and emotions.

LITTLE MARY

I have solid memories of Little Mary, who was almost three years older than I was. She was the first light in my meadow. I remember playing with her and

Mary and Steve as children.

helping her and Grandma wash dishes. I had to stand on a chair to reach the dishes when Mary was seven and I was four. She was a girl, so I felt comfortable being around her. I didn't recognize her as my aunt at that time, but I knew she was my grandparents' child—she called them Mom and Dad—but I didn't make that connection then. I just knew I liked being around Mary because she treated me with loving kindness. I got very close to her. She understood well before I did that I was her nephew, and I felt safe when I was around her, even though we were both kids.

DENISE

As I was the first grandchild on my dad's side of the family, I sensed a lot of family expectations went along with that. My cousin Denise was next to me in line. She was her own person, with a strong personality, and fun to be around. She was then and today remains a beautiful free spirit, living life on her terms, embracing her personality. Wanting to be more like her, I would observe her. I was aware of her confidence and energy. I loved her so much and was proud to know her not just as my cousin but also as my friend. My relationship with Denise remains as beautiful as it was when we were kids. She is always there with her smile and vivaciousness, never letting the world get her down. I love who she is. I knew I couldn't be her—girls had a vastly different way of living. It seemed to me that not as much was expected of them back then. She was my second light in my meadow.

JOHNNY

My cousin Johnny was my third light. Johnny was a mild-mannered, laid-back kid. Being easygoing and nonthreatening, he had his own brand of confidence going on. I sensed his energy and instinctively felt he was somewhat of a loner, as was I, so we were close. Like Denise, he and I were consistent with our bond, which remains to this day.

MY LIGHTS

I didn't know at the time, but what I was creating with the lights in my mind was a gathering of people I trusted. The lights metaphor wasn't created until a little later. I didn't call them my lights; they were people I felt comfortable with and would always gravitate toward. These few family members meant a lot to me and still do to this day. I will forever love them for their acts of acceptance back then. They are kind people who look for the good in others, as I do.

THINGS CHANGED

On my mom's side, I was the fourth oldest out of five boys born within a two-year period. Two of my cousins and I were the same age, born just a month apart from one another. I felt close to them, and as we grew up, that bond stayed. Both of them were somewhat laid-back too, taking life as it came. When we were little, things were good. I was shier and more reserved than all my cousins.

As I got older, things changed, especially with my mom's side of the family. My aunts and uncles started to recognize that I was a quiet kid, gentle with life in general. I liked to talk and be inside the house. I didn't really like getting dirty or talking about the things boys talked about at those ages. The older adults began noticing things that set me apart from the other boys I was being raised with. The other cousins didn't really say too much, but I remember one incident where all five of us boys were walking into the house with my aunt ahead of us. She held the door for the first four, and as I was approaching the door, she looked at me in disgust and then shut the door. She didn't hold it for me. This probably wasn't much to someone else, but for me, it was a defining moment. It epitomized what had already begun in my life in school and at home. It added to me not feeling accepted or equal, and I was intuitive enough that I knew some of the family saw me with disgust. It was a time when judgments, cliques, and discrimination were alive and well. It got to the point where I dreaded visiting Mom's side of the family, which eventually totaled twenty-one kids. My siblings and I had thirty-one first cousins when both families were combined. There were thirteen of us in my generation who grew up together; the remaining five on my dad's side were born after most of us were on our own.

My aunts on my mother's side of the family noticed that I didn't want to play with the four boy cousins and would rather play quietly by myself. My socializing wasn't going according to the norms that were set. Knowing that I was vastly different from these cousins, I started to withdraw. I was reminded harshly that I was different. They tried to shame me into playing with the other boys, and then I would cry because I was being forced with shaming words. My parents could see it too. They saw in me the timid, kind, gentle self I was becoming. No one on either side of the family had a boy who was quite like me. Even though Johnny was laid-back, he still liked being outside, getting dirty, and doing things boys did. I didn't like cars, and instead of hating girls, I embraced them. Most of them were my kind of people; they were softer and gentler to play with. My mom and dad were likely out of their element, dealing with a kid like me. I know my boy cousins on my mom's side sensed it too. It didn't help that a few of my aunts went along with the boys. The aunts would always choose the other boys to go do things with and left me out. After a while, I didn't want to go because I would be singled out and made to feel uncomfortable.

This is when my confidence started to diminish and my self-worth was impacted. I would cry because my feelings were hurt. This is the single most important element that set me apart from all the boys and adults, and I knew it. Boys weren't supposed to be sensitive and emotional. I was starting to be treated differently. I can't remember what I did on one particular day, but Aunt Agnes, my dad's aunt, told me I should have been a girl when I was about nine or ten. She was the first person to call me a sissy. This woman was sort of mean. I remember feeling threatened when I was around her.

I found that being around the girls was easier for me. I felt it. I was a very sensitive boy, and I recognized that in them as well. They were my tribe, so to speak. Being a sensitive boy at that young age, I knew I had a difficult, emotionally filled future ahead of me. My feelings could be hurt easily, and I cried in situations when I felt someone was being mean or misunderstood me.

Looking back on this, I don't really know how my parents coped with that. I remember my mom telling me to shut up when I cried. My dad would just walk away, shaking his head. Dad was a farmer, and although he had a gentle spirit, as he raised his family, he wanted his boys to be more like him. I think I embarrassed him. I started to gravitate more toward my mom. I could feel the strength and strictness with some softness in her, and I trusted I would be protected. I needed to be protected. I was a kinder, gentler person. My dad could not relate to me, sensing my difference, and he gravitated toward my brother, closest to me in age. My brother and Dad had farming in common. I did not. Naturally, Dad's connection with him developed, and he picked up everything Dad did. He looked forward to working the fields and being a farmer and all that went with that. I was a bit relieved as the pressure for me was shifted, but I also knew that I would be shunned and treated badly because I wasn't doing farming duties and being like the rest of the boys in that area. This set the stage for the rest of my growing years. Looking back on those years, I think if I would have been encouraged to build up my confidence, I could have been a good field worker. I like straight lines, uniformity, starting and accomplishing a task. I like the way a field looks when it's plowed or planted. I would have been good at treating these fields as pieces of art.

I didn't know it then, but I was gay. I didn't realize it or couldn't understand it; I didn't know the name for my difference, the person I was becoming. I knew without a doubt I didn't like to farm because of the lack of confidence. The machinery intimidated me to the point I was scared to use them. If I did try to drive, I was made fun of or yelled at if a mistake was made. One of the only aspects I liked about farming was taking care of the animals, the cows and pigs. The sounds, smells, and scenery were all beautiful to me. Sometimes we would go pick up eggs with my grandparents, gathering eggs at the huge chicken house. They probably had somewhere around 9,000 chickens. Believe it or not, my cousins and I looked forward to going with my grandparents to gather eggs, which were sold to local markets. Eggs were picked up twice a day, with 5,000 to 6,000 eggs picked each time.

Everyone I knew lived in the country and worked on their farms. I couldn't relate to others because I didn't talk about farming, or girls, or the things my friends did, or even what adults talked about. That's all they knew. I would find comfort in the house, reading and writing. I liked climbing to the top of the tree in the backyard because it was a great place to think. It became a safe haven for me. I knew I was going to have a hard existence because of the way I was. My strength to maintain my core stayed, and I relied on it. Even in pain, I stayed true to myself the only way I knew how to at that time. I only had confidence in being me, and at times, even that was shaky.

Little Mary showed me support and love from the beginning. I can't remember her words, but I do remember feeling loved and supported by her. She was more like an older sister. I recognized her presence in my life at that young age, and I trusted her. Having Mary was a godsend and still is today. She was my first friend. Her presence in our family was a gift from the Universe. I used to look forward to going to Grandma and Grandpa's house to be around her. Sometimes I would spend the night at my grandparents' house; I'm not sure why, but maybe to give Mom and Dad a break after they had twin babies. One morning after waking from a night's sleep on the couch in my grandparents' living room, I noticed pieces of cushion stuffing around on the floor. I asked my grandpa what that was, and he told me that mice were running around the house overnight and on top of me to get cushion stuffing for their nests. Mary laughed and said, "Don't worry, Steven, they didn't get on you." I had been wide-eyed listening to my grandpa. He got a real kick out of it. I must have looked petrified. Later, I thought it was funny too.

When I started school, Mary was already in the fourth grade at Cedar Bluff Elementary School in Fults, Illinois. My first-grade class had about twenty-two kids in it. Cedar Bluff was a small school designed and built especially for the kids from the outlying farming community to help with the transition to Valmeyer where the high school was located. It took the stress off the district and the kids to have us go to school at Cedar Bluff through the fifth grade then transfer us to Valmeyer in sixth grade.

First grade was a tidal wave of fear for me, but that is where I had to learn to stand on my own. I cried quite a bit when Mom dropped me off that first day. She waited in the hall until I stopped, but it took a while. I was small in stature and looked young even by first-grade standards. I was an emotional kid who felt things deeply. The only socialization I'd had up to this point was with a few cousins with whom I was raised. I had no choice, so I went into the classroom and met my teacher. She was a tall, very thin lady who wore a dress. She was polite and very kind to me. Little did I know she was conditioning me to leave Mom in the hallway. So I went with her kindness, as I gravitated toward women anyway. She sat me down at the little table where other kids were playing. She said to me, "Here is some Play-Doh; play with this until you feel comfortable to play with the other kids. Until that happens, you play here." The kid next to me saw the little dog I had made with my Play-Doh. He then grabbed it and ate the head off my dog. I was mortified looking at him as he was chewing it. The teacher saw what he had done and stood him in the corner. My teacher was such a nice lady. I will never forget her kindness. Being sensitive around the other boys and girls was pretty bad. The name "sissy" came at me again, this time like a wreckingball in

Steve in first grade, 1968.

the face. Some of the other boys, many of whom had older siblings were conditioned to being picked on, bullied, or whatever. I was not used to such a world or that kind of behavior.

So it was that at the age of six, my psyche started changing. I decided to like a girl, even though I knew I didn't want to have a girlfriend, because I was being picked on so badly. I kissed a girl, and my teacher stood me in the corner. Getting in trouble further eroded any confidence I may have had, and I started to spiral downward into a pit I wouldn't be able to climb out of for a long time. It marked the beginning of me losing myself.

I kissed that girl to show the boys I liked girls and keep them from picking on me. It backfired. Having to stand in the corner for all to see was humiliating. I wasn't supposed to kiss a girl. I was supposed to hate them, but I didn't. I began losing what little confidence and self-esteem I had, but I realized in some part of my soul that I was in only in the first grade; I had a long way to go to grow up.

I was picked on even harder because of this incident. The boys in my class— not all of them, just a few with low self-esteem and no confidence—picked on me. They were the bullies that would be with me the entire time I attended school. I had two friends I would hang out with at recess and stayed by them most of those grade school years.

Later that year, two girls wanted to show me some pet rabbits at their house, so I went with them after school. Without telling anyone, I got on their bus. I think I knew this was wrong, but in desperate need of being liked, I went with them to the one girl's house. The bus driver didn't seem to question them when they said they were taking me home. Well, that started a bad thing. The girl's dad questioned her about where I came from and who I was. Mom saw the bus drive by our house and not stop to let me off, so she freaked out. I found out later that she and my mom's sister, who lived across the field from us and was also my godmother, took off looking for me. They found me, and boy, did I get a spanking. Mom went to the school board and raised a lot of hell and had the school put a security system in place with notes the kids had to carry so the bus drivers knew if another kid was supposed to take a different bus. She insisted on the new policy for the whole school district, and it was adopted because of what I did. Thinking back, I now know where my ability to stand up for change comes from. It started with my mom. The spanking I received was deserved. I was destined to make changes. It was the beginning of becoming creative to survive.

3 : Become the Change You Want to See

My empathic abilities were revealed at a very young age. I was called a sissy again, this time by some boys in the class. To this day, when I hear someone calling another a sissy, I lose respect for the person saying it and stand up for the person it's being said to. Sissy is a very derogatory name used by bullies to make someone feel weak. It's degrading and should never be used.

I had already developed a crush on one of my friends and knew inside that I really liked him. There is a school picture in which I am standing up very straight but so close to him that you almost couldn't see between us. When I brought the picture home, my dad asked, "Why are you standing so close to that boy?'"

I hadn't thought anything of it because I didn't know how to define my feelings. When asked, I just said, "He is my friend, and I like him." I look back on that now and kind of laugh a little. I'm sure my mom and dad were beside themselves many times when it came to how I acted. It had to have been a shock for them to witness behaviors that were unique to me.

I was picked on relentlessly; I lacked the courage to fight back. I just wanted people to like me. I saw myself as a likable kid with a nice smile. I thought if I showed people how friendly I was through my smile, it would be enough. It wasn't.

My parents were both strong and everyone liked them. Neither of them lacked confidence. I'm sure they found me to be embarrassing, to say the least. I don't know how they coped with that. The other boys in my class picked up on me being more sensitive than most kids, and the torment never stopped. The boys who were insecure with a bully complex were the ones who picked on me. Naturally, the girls saw me as a sweet boy, someone they could be friends with who wouldn't be mean to them or threatening. I understood basic feelings and emotions in myself and in the girls and a few of the boys.

Mom and Dad knew I wasn't like the other boys. It upset them when I talked about being picked on. I felt humiliated and stopped talking about it, as I could feel my parents' sadness and disgust. This is when my life changed. I crawled inside my protective world. Unfortunately, it almost seemed like Mom and Dad thought if they treated me mean and judged me, that it would make me tougher, as if they wanted me to be a thoughtless, unkind boy. My siblings picked up on it and started treating me with disrespect and being mean to me with no regard for my personal space. They didn't understand what Mom and Dad were trying to do, but I did. It created a humiliating and unloving environment for me, which reverberated throughout both sides of my family, as Dad would talk about it to his family and Mom would talk about it with hers. Many people I grew up with would jump on that hate bandwagon and treat me horribly. My confidence, self-esteem, and every bit of my being was being challenged and taken away.

I remember my grandpa telling my dad I should have been a girl, in the house wearing a dress, just because I couldn't even drive a tractor correctly. He was right about the tractor. I almost hit a hog house while I was driving the tractor. Dad was on one fender, Grandpa on the other. I jumped off the tractor when I got it back to the house while it was still moving and hid inside crying. I felt worthless, even though I knew I wasn't. These were people who were supposed to love me; I couldn't understand why they didn't. I didn't take criticism well because I looked at the world with a kind heart and was devastated when someone was mean to me. I wasn't mean to anyone and couldn't understand why anyone would treat me badly. I took it seriously, and it went deep into my psyche. I couldn't understand why anyone would be mean and hateful, and yet, this is how my world looked and how I was treated. Not just kids my age, but even the adults were against me because I wasn't following their version of what normal was to them. I could feel the separation, knowing I didn't fit in, so I remained on the fringe. I understood the adults thought I was bringing shame to my mom and dad.

I didn't have anyone to look to for support except Little Mary and (Aunt) Big Mary, who would try to build me up as they saw what was happening. Looking back on this now, I am astonished no one else came to my rescue. I guess these two aunts were the only ones who could see and understood my personality and the outlook I had on life.

It was difficult because I couldn't escape the torment. So, I escaped to my safe place at the top of the tree in our backyard. I would climb to the top of it and look out across the bottoms, wondering what was on the other side of the bluffs visible in the distance. I would sit up there for hours daydreaming about leaving all these hateful people and figuring out how to simply survive growing up while dreading the next day. I can still see the beautiful blue sky, green fields, and a haze that shadowed the bluffs in the distance from the hot summer days and feel the breeze moving the leaves around me. An occasional bird would land on the tree, and I'm sure they wondered what I was doing there. I could smell the freshly tilled dirt from the farmers working the fields. I loved climbing to the top of that tree and hiding from the world. I was out of sight, but I could hear my siblings running around on the ground playing. Once in a while, I could hear them yell my name. I never answered. When no one was around, I climbed down from that tree so my safe place would remain secret.

I realized early on that my mind was pretty powerful and that it would help me navigate through life. I developed a keen sense of when dangerous people were around. It was a survival sense I developed by living with my siblings and surviving abuse from the kids I went to school with and some of my cousins. I trained myself to observe and read people quickly. It meant survival to me. I came up with a profound survival technique while sitting at the top of that tree.

MY LIGHTS

I was about ten or eleven years old when I knew there was something different about me. I never told anyone because my survival depended on it. The feeling of isolation and of not being good enough was enough to make me think I wanted to end my existence. I was completely sad and lonely. I was made to feel worthless, unlovable, and that there was something wrong with me. I started feeling like I wouldn't survive because I was just a kid, and I had a long way to go before I could grow up and leave. I had some very dark moments. I didn't know if I wanted to keep living. I don't know where this thought came from, but it did, and I just kept it to myself. I never told anyone.

As I got older, I made a few friends outside my family, and it was wonderful having people who liked me for me, even though there weren't many. One time I overheard a few of my aunts talking about envisioning a meadow with flowers covering it as a nice place to go when they wanted to escape and daydream about something beautiful.

I thought, "That's a nice idea." Realizing I needed light, I turned my friends into little lights. They became lights in my life where before was only emptiness, loneliness, and darkness. I put them in the meadow to replace the flowers. To me, they were more beautiful than the flowers because of what they represented. As I grew, I would gradually add more lights to my meadow. I was thankful and appreciated each of the lights. I took comfort in those little lights, knowing that I wasn't damaged and there wasn't anything terrible about me, that there were people who liked me as I was. My friends and my lights became part of the secrets I kept.

With my feelings and thoughts, my friends, my secret place, and my secret lights in the meadow, I was able to keep myself somewhat safe. I was the change I wanted to see in others.

4 : The Beginning of Awareness

One day I was in our bathroom, looking out the window at the yard below, when I felt a rush, as if there were energy in the room. That's when I became aware that I was more attracted to boys than to girls. I wasn't that old, but I knew in my being that it was true. My memory of that moment is as vivid as if it had just happened. I remember thinking how hard it was going to be for me, growing up in a bigoted area where not that many people were open-minded. I was petrified with the realization of knowing this about myself. I knew that if anyone found out about me, it would be the end. It was almost as if I couldn't breathe. The fear was indescribable.

I was only ten years old when a redheaded girl, a year younger than me, sent a note, which I was reading in the car.

I had flirted with the idea of having a girlfriend, thinking it would cover up the person inside that I was trying to hide. This girl and I remained close growing up, and she was added to my meadow of lights. This little image I had created in my head helped me to cope. I knew I had a lot of potential and was decently smart—smart enough to know that I had to keep hiding parts of who I was in order to survive. As it was, most everyone thought I was weak, a sissy, and didn't deserve their respect. The beauty was that I didn't respect them either. Why would I want their respect? I saw how they treated me and each other.

That summer marked my transition into sixth grade and a new school. This was my second abrupt introduction to new kids, as my class merged with kids the same age in Valmeyer. I was terrified of meeting new kids again. I must have gone into it numb.

Even at this young age, I never could understand why people were picked on. Later, I realized that not everyone is secure with who they are and used bullying tactics to feel better about themselves. I was aware of myself as being a decent person not hurting anyone, always leading with my smile, hoping I would be received in a friendly way. The thought of intentionally hurting someone never entered my mind. I liked everyone.

It wasn't until I reached sixth grade at Valmeyer that my life turned into real hell. I wasn't in a small country school anymore. My world and the kids I attended first through fifth grade with all changed drastically, as twenty more were added to us, new boys and girls who grouped together. Their cliques ensured no one could get close. The marginalization was a group effort, since they saw themselves at the top of the class hierarchy. They defined the limits, drew the lines. The kids in my class from Cedar Bluff who had tormented me aligned themselves with the same attitudes and arrogance that these new kids displayed, which meant they were accepted and included into the cliques. They bullied not just me, but other kids fell prey too. In a way, that was a form of protection because their sights weren't always on me. *Sissy* continued to be my moniker. Threats of being beat up persisted, but gratefully, that never happened.

I managed to make a few friends (lights). I remember a friend who sat behind me in class and how her eye twitched. I asked her what that was. She said it happened when she got hungry. I was amazed at that. I think of that once in a while and laugh a little.

My dad planned a hayride in the summer between my eighth grade and freshman years with my sister and brothers and kids from Prairie du Rocher, another country town. I had a date with a girl. She wanted to kiss me, so I kissed her. She wanted to make out, but I said I didn't want to because, as

I told her, "I don't want to get you pregnant." I was so naïve. I hadn't been taught anything, and no one shared stories with me. I just said that to her. Word got back to people and that was the beginning of new torment for me. But I knew those people didn't know any better about sex. Still, I stayed upstairs the whole next day, afraid of coming down so they could make fun of me. I could hear them talking about me. It was awful. I didn't know anything as everything was kept from me, even trying to learn different music groups.

One afternoon in the summer, I overheard people at my house talking about musical groups. I wasn't allowed to be in the same room with them, so I eavesdropped and wrote down the names of the groups they were talking about so I could feel I knew something too. They talked about REO Speedwagon. Well…I heard and wrote it down as "Oreo." One of them came in, snatched my paper, took it back, and they all laughed at me. Even though I was the oldest, I had no standing and was not looked at with any sort of respect.

I know, it's not unusual to get picked on, but this felt so deliberate. I was constantly singled out. Maybe it would have been different if they picked on each other, but they didn't. I was isolated. It was always my three siblings against me. They let me know I didn't fit.

On a deep level, I was so lost trying to figure out what to do, who to be, and how to act. I grew up alone in my own home. I was never included, except to be blamed for stuff. And, of course, my parents believed them.

"You're the oldest," I was told. "You should have known better and not shown them something to get them in trouble." Living at home was difficult for me. Now I can see they had deep emotional issues with their own identities, but it was all put on me so they wouldn't have to examine themselves. They had to be better than anyone else, which meant sacrificing me so they could look better. My entire youth was surrounded by this behavior and cruel treatment—not with just my family, but with many of the people I knew. Feeling their relentless hatred, I withdrew even further. I wanted to be invisible.

I went to summer school many summers because I couldn't stay focused in school and my grades suffered with all the torment I was put through. I had no self-confidence. But I figured out I knew that there would be fewer kids to be around in summer school, and the kids I was with in summer school were also shunned to a certain degree. I passed summer school each year and advanced to the next grade. Also, summer school was only four to six weeks long, so I was still able to enjoy my summers. Little did I know then that going to summer school would be an asset in my senior year.

I was aware of the little things that brought me peace. I have some very heart-warming memories from growing up in the country. I would love waking up on a summer morning, smelling the summer breeze as it wafted through the bedroom window. With everyone still asleep, I had peace, and my mind would fly to dreams I had for myself. I could smell the coffee and breakfast Mom was preparing for Dad, sometimes eggs and bacon, or ham. There was always a good smell wafting up the stairs. I could hear them talking about what was going to be done for that day.

I would go to sleep at night with the sounds of a far-off train whistle, dogs barking, or pigs in the pen lifting the metal lids to get their food then dropping them, which sounded wonderful to me. Otherwise, it was quiet, and looking out the window, I could see the stars from my bed, which made me dream about what was out in the world. I would fall asleep feeling peaceful, slightly content. I saw and appreciated the beauty of the little things life offered.

I used to really enjoy watching the plants sprout and then grow after Dad had planted the crops. The fields would be a solid sheet of green as far as the eye could see, and as I stared at them, I found myself at ease. There were times when we would have some very dry summers, waiting for the rains to come so the fields could grow. Mom and Dad believed in prayer, so when this would happen, they would get us out of bed at night and take us downstairs. Dad said, "Kids, we need to pray for the rains to come," and we would all kneel down next to the couch and pray. I remember, we each prayed hard, saying the prayers out loud for the rains to come. It was one of the few tender moments that stood out for me. Rain eventually came. Whether the prayers helped or not, they did come. I liked being part of the family for this.

An old wooden single-car garage sat near the house, sort of across the yard from our house. It was leaning to one side, barely standing, as the wood was becoming too weak to hold it up. Dad and Mom wanted to remove it so it wouldn't fall down and hurt any of us. Dad took his John Deere and pushed it over, so it was in a heap on the ground.

I heard him tell Mom, "Now I have to make time to clean that up."

I somehow knew I could clean this up for him. I remember getting a hammer and a crowbar and taking nails out of the wood, freeing it so I could stack it in neat and orderly piles. I dismantled that shed piece by piece, including the tin sheets that covered the roof. My mom and dad observed me taking it apart. When I had completed my task, I had all the wood stacked neatly, including the dismantled rafters. I'd filled a bucket full of nails so they weren't lying around to puncture tires or toes. And the tin sheets were stacked neatly in piles.

Dad came home from working in the fields and bragged to Mom about the job I did for him. That was when I discovered how my brain worked—in an organized, methodical manner. I liked to arrange and organize things and keep them orderly.

When we went to my grandparents' house after church that Sunday, Dad bragged to them, saying, "Steven took that entire shed apart, stacked all the pieces in piles. All I had to do was call the neighbor to come and get it. I was happy he did this for me. I couldn't believe what I saw with what he did." I was proud of what I had done too and cherished the moment he bragged about me. It was a moment I could help him out without going into the fields.

I was a precocious kid and felt things deeply. Not only was I able to feel, but even better, I could read people. I would sometimes ignore what I saw and go with what I thought would be liked for making a new friend. I found out quickly that I was right about my instinct, but I ignored them because I wanted to be liked. I was being raised with people who showed me that I shouldn't like them in the first place. I was looking for validation and something to make me feel worthy, but even then, I knew it had to come from people who didn't have a clue how to be decent or have empathy in the first place. Getting a little bit of validation from Dad made me realize how much I needed it from others, but I usually didn't get it. I became even more solitary, if that was even possible.

5 : The Ones Who Saw Me

Never underestimate the power of intuition. An intuitive person recognizes your game even before you play it. Trust your instincts; intuition doesn't lie.

As I got older, the pressure of working on the farm increased to the point where it would make me sick. Mom got tired of me hanging around the house and not doing anything. I was doing something, though: I was being me. The idea of me working on the farm with Dad, driving the tractors and all that, was not in my being. I didn't want to have something else added to my list of failures that people could use against me. I couldn't bear anymore failures. I didn't want to work on the farm, which drove a wedge between Dad and me and widened the distance I had already been feeling. It seemed to take on a different tone, which I felt for the rest of my growing years.

My brother, next to me in age, was a clone of Dad. Dad would take him to work outside over me all the time. I would complain even though I didn't want to do it, but I wasn't jealous of my brother who loved farming. Massive machinery scared me, and I didn't have the confidence to even try learning it.

Sissy became synonymous with Steven. I was labeled and put inside the proverbial box, and I couldn't get out of it. Depressed and frightened, I went through the motions of trying to survive the best way I could and stay as far under the radar as possible. The only thing I could count on was my own mind and thoughts. The idea of growing up and leaving was scary and too far away, so I pushed it aside, only dreaming about it when I was at the top of my tree. Somehow, I knew there would be people out in the world who would appreciate a guy like me and whom I would appreciate too. I just had to be patient. Little did I know that when I got older, sheer desperation would force me to make a change.

Along with a few members on my dad's side of the family, my godmother, Mom's sister, saw the goodness in me too. She would make me feel special when she was around. She and my uncle and their kids, my cousins, lived across the field from us. They were farmers too. We all grew up together. They were closer to me than anyone else on Mom's side of the family. Dana, the eldest, eventually married an Air Force man. She and I have remained close throughout our lives. Her sister joined the Air Force after I was already in, and their youngest son joined the Army. Dana remains a confidant of mine and I am hers. It's easy to talk with Dana, and like Little Mary, she knows my past and what I went through. They were among the brightest lights in my meadow.

Looking back, it's amazing to me that most people didn't care enough about me to talk with me or try to understand where I was emotionally. I felt like almost everyone I went to school with talked about me, listened to each other, and made up things about me to further berate me. I cared more about what people thought of me than what I thought of myself. This was my downfall. I could see that most of the people around me had their own level of issues too. People assumed I wouldn't amount to much. The sad thing about this is, I started to feel that way too because of it. I couldn't focus because I was always on guard. Little Mary was about the only one I could really go to and talk with about my feelings and what was happening. She could see what was happening too. I could read her. Eventually, I didn't say too much to her because I felt like I was making her very sad, and she didn't know what to do anyway. I could feel Mary loved me, and I knew, without a doubt, that's where my empathy came from for her. She could see I was being hurt, and since she loved me, that hurt her. I didn't want to hurt her like that, so I started to keep things to myself.

High school was like walking through a dungeon; danger lurked around every corner, especially when I was in Physical Education and had to take a shower with all those boys, being picked on and naked. That was absolutely the worst.

6 : It Was Coming From Me

I am the energy that influences my world.

During our freshman year, my friend Danny started calling me Tigger. This was a nickname that I liked, and after a while, it actually stuck tighter than sissy. To my delight, a few boys wanted to be my friend. I was cautious, but I let them in, and I ended up trusting them and they became lights too. Danny was a friend (light) to me, and later in life, I found out he was also gay. Danny was stronger than me and was out to himself, but we never talked about it in school because it would have been too dangerous, as we could have been beaten up or been bullied even more. Later in life, he told me he knew I was gay in high school, which I thought was pretty cool. I couldn't even think about my own sexuality as it was too much to bear given the scrutiny I was living daily. Danny was picked on too; not as much, but he was. One day, in chorus, the seniors were picking on him. He and I sat next to each other as tenors, with the senior boys behind us. They really picked on him badly. They didn't touch me because Mary was also a senior, and she would have laid into them. One day, Danny had had enough, and he swung his arm around, clipping me on the side of the eye, which hurt like crazy. Danny stood up and said he had had enough and threw over a chair to get out and run into the hallway. Mary asked if I was OK. I was tearing up but didn't cry as my emotional control was getting stronger. Mary and our music teacher took me into the hallway where Danny was to make sure we were OK. Danny's anger was so powerful, it startled me. Mary went back in the classroom, and I could hear her yelling at those boys, saying something along the lines of, "You mess with my nephew, you mess with me."

Soon after this came my first intuition about Mom and Dad I could feel something was going to happen because I paid attention to their behaviors and energy. Even though everyone thought I was meek and didn't know anything, I understood feelings and emotions pretty deeply and could read them easily in others. I didn't talk much, but I observed others and kept it to myself.

I had Mom and Dad on my mind and was so upset thinking about their situation, I broke down in study hall one day and started crying heavily. I couldn't take life any longer. I was under pressure everywhere and had no place to turn. In study hall, I asked to have Little Mary come see me. I ended up being so distraught that she took me home. I stayed home with Mom and told her what was happening.

Mom said to me, "You don't need to worry about your dad and me." The trouble was, I could feel what they were feeling; my empathic ways were developing and gaining strength. I look back on some of this and realized I was more developed on the emotional side of things than I thought. I was way ahead of anyone I was growing up with at that time. Feeling and being sensitive to emotions were valuable for me.

The way society viewed boys versus girls was (and remains) very skewed. Boys weren't supposed to be sensitive, caring, and gentle. The unhealthy expectations placed on males in American society create dysfunction. Growing up with man-made, biased social expectations was so difficult, I considered suicide. It's clear to me why gay kids—or any kids who don't fit into the expected profile—too often fulfill their suicidal thoughts. It's also unfair for straight boys to have to suppress their sensitivity, which leads to anger, violence, addictions, and sometimes suicide as well. It is overwhelming to deal with alone. Raising a strong boy to be a man is very misunderstood in this country.

Being strong-willed, I knew I had a lot to offer the world if I met my potential and was able to be myself. I loved myself way more than anyone else did and stayed true to my feelings and emotions. Still, living daily with the relentless insults and derogatory comments was demoralizing. I cried a lot at the top of that tree. My feelings were being hurt so much by people who were supposed to love me that depression started to creep into my psyche. I carved my name in the tree to remind me that this was my place, and that *Steve was a decent guy.* I would look at my name carved in the tree and think, "This is my name. No one else in my family has it, but what does it mean to them other than embarrassment?" I started to hate my name because it was so often associated with laughter and insults.

The thought of growing up and leaving was a constant for me. I just had to be patient and stay out of sight as much as I could. I still had a long way to go to be an adult and wasn't sure I could make it. The saddest thing about all this is no one thought I would amount to anything because they saw me as useless, weak, emotional, and a sissy. My perception of myself was the complete opposite. I knew my qualities and would never exchange them just to fit in or be mean to anyone. I think that is the worst anyone could do to someone. I persevered because I was able to see how dysfunctional everyone around me behaved.

I was so desperate to have people like me that if anyone gave me the slightest attention, I was glued to them then. A girl in my class was nice to me one day. I thought this was a chance for me to be accepted, so I started to show her I liked her. I wanted her to be my girlfriend. Many of the other boys were getting girlfriends, and I thought if I could get one, then the marginalizing would stop. I pursued her in a misguided, stalking, mishap sort of way. I was like an unguided electrical impulse. I didn't know what I was doing. I would write her letters expressing my love for her and would call her on occasion and talk nonsense, the whole time having no confidence in myself.

School had begun again after the summer break, and my infatuation with her increased. One day I saw her talking with another boy and laughing and stuff. My emotional issues surfaced. I wrote a terrible letter about that boy and posted it on the bulletin board in the hallway. One of my classmates came into the study hall where I was sitting and told me how stupid I was and how stupid that letter was. It was yet another embarrassing moment for me, a moment I created, putting myself in line with their radar instead of under it. This reinforced the image people had of me as something damaged and a sissy. It never would have occurred to them that it was because of them I was in this emotional state of mind.

I went home, straight to the top of the tree, and cried hard, not even taking into consideration that what I had done was awful. I didn't take ownership of it. I looked at it as if no one cared what I said in the letter; they only looked at what I did, not the reason why I did it. That is the issue that I couldn't see. I didn't know how to tap into my own strength on that level. Looking back on this now, I had confirmed what they were making me believe about myself. Everyone had to be the same, act the same, wear the same things, talk, look, and think the same, never stepping up as individuals. To them, being normal was to be like each other. Very Stepford-like living. The mid 1970s was a hodgepodge of alcohol, infidelity, judgments, drugs, and abusive behaviors; however, everyone went to church.

I'm laughing as I think about the hypocrisy. I never believed in organized religion, and these realizations drove that home to me. It didn't make sense and it didn't appeal to people like me. The institution itself didn't like or want people like me anyway.

Mom and Dad ended up divorcing. The reasons why they were divorcing were clear to me, as I had witnessed and heard most everything that was being said. I was so worried about them, I would run downstairs and be with them. My parents' personalities were very different, and the level of confidence in each of them was conflicting. I could see for some years where their marriage was headed. I was right; they separated. One of the few times I was treated as the eldest was when Mom and Dad had to go to court for the divorce and to decide custody and child support issues. The judge asked to have the oldest child come in to sit on the bench so he could ask me some questions. Of all the times to have me live my role as the eldest, this was the most frightening. Mom welcomed that time. She knew I wouldn't lie, and I didn't. I remember that setting as vividly as if it had happened yesterday. With my parents looking at me from their chairs—Dad and his girlfriend down on my left with his lawyer, and Mom and her lawyer down on my right—I took the oath on the Bible. I looked down toward the floor from an elevated platform next to the judge, who asked me who I thought we should stay with.

"Our mom," I said.

"Why?" he asked. I said, "Because she is stronger than Dad when it comes to keeping us in line. If we went to Dad's, my siblings wouldn't listen to him. They don't have the discipline and intelligence to do the right thing and would run over him. We wouldn't have structure in our lives. Mom is stronger. We will have a stable home life with her."

"Are your parents dating anyone?" he asked.

"Mom isn't." Then I pointed at Dad's girlfriend sitting next to him. I said, "Dad's girlfriend is sitting next to him."

The judge asked me if I saw Dad and his girlfriend sleeping together, and I said yes. Their bedroom is at the bottom of the stairs where we go past to get to the kitchen and the rest of the house. The judge asked if I ever saw any naked parts. I said, "Once I saw her boob." I know I hurt my dad because I could see it in his face, but he also knew I was telling the truth.

In the outer hallway, my siblings were trying to listen through the door, but my aunts were there, pulling them back. With my testimony, the judge said that we would stay with Mom as the primary parent.

There was one thing I didn't tell anyone. I knew if Dad took us from Mom, she wouldn't have survived. Her mental state was being pummeled and her confidence assaulted due to the divorce. Needless to say, this further divided my dad from me. He didn't talk with me for about a year, and my siblings went into high gear treating me badly, fueled by my dad telling them what I had done. When word got out about what I had done, it seemed the whole community on the farming side of things turned their backs on me even more. Still, I knew I did the right thing, and that was all that mattered to me.

Eventually, Dad and I reconciled. We spent every other weekend at my dad's house from the time I was sixteen until I graduated. As usual, I kept to myself.

Mom was awarded one of the farms in the divorce, my dad the other. We stayed with Mom on the farm for a few years after the divorce, but the winters got to be too much for her. Our water pump would freeze, so she and I would go to the barn, deep in the night, when it was cold and often snowy, and I would climb down in the hole to put on the heat lamp so our pipes wouldn't freeze. Even walking to catch the school bus in the morning down our lane was hard, having to climb over snow drifts. Our lane was around a thousand feet to the main road. It was a good distance for four young kids to walk in conditions like that, but we had no other choice.

Mom sought advice and sold the farmhouse and five acres. She bought a house in Red Bud. Mom is a survivor and knows how to make things work out.

Once again, I was confronted with a whole new set of school kids. I was petrified, going from a class of forty-three to a class of nearly two hundred. I'd finally learned where the dangers were in Valmeyer, but in Red Bud, I had no idea. Unbeknownst to me, I had enough credits transferred from Valmeyer because of summer school that I didn't have to go to school full-time in Red Bud. That was a surprising silver lining.

I thought I would try to like another girl, as no one knew me at this school, but I was immediately rejected. The kids in this new school talked about each other, and before I knew it everyone was shunning me. The shaming ensued. I couldn't understand why no one wanted me around or thought I was interesting enough to try to get to know. Even though no one knew me at this school, I got the same insults.

What I didn't know at that time, and what it took a long time to learn, was that it all came from me. I was putting out insecure energy. People could sense my lack of confidence and observe the way I acted. I'd had enough. I stood in the bathtub in our bathroom, looking for a way to end my life. I was crying so hard, looking at myself in the mirror, wondering what was so terrible about me that no one liked me. Fortunately, I cried it out and the thought of ending my life passed. I released the feeling and emotions by crying, so that when I was done, even though nothing was healed, I felt a bit better.

The Universe put a friend in my path soon after this. Jana, a quiet, timid girl, wanted to be my friend. She became another light in my life. She could see me and became a friend of mine quickly. She was sent to me from the Universe when I needed a kind, understanding human the most.

Having just written that, I realize I didn't know enough to understand the Universe and what power it held. Much later, I discovered that the Universe puts people, things, and situations in our path to change, protect, and lead us in the way we are meant to go. I didn't have the confidence or self-awareness to see what I needed to do to grow. The Universe sent me Jana and Cindy and a neighbor boy to help change the path I was on. These friends helped me begin developing a sense of who I was, of my value and essence.

It helped knowing I was closer to being eighteen and could leave. I still didn't have a plan for what I was going to do. I just knew I was going to get out of there. I was in fear of the unknown, but that fear didn't measure up to what I had lived through to that point. I was about to take a risk in a big way. I had no choice but to look for an opportunity to leave. Those days of daydreaming stayed fresh in my mind. I had added strength and determination, a resolute energy. I was about to graduate from high school.

7 : I'm Not Alone

I paid attention and observed people and situations coming into my life. I started to be keenly aware of who I was.

Even though I was unhappy, I always believed in myself. I knew I had a lot to offer the world. The world I'd grown up in didn't think of me that way or could even see me for who I was, but I held onto my belief in myself and knew it was up to me, and no one else, to make a change. I also knew that I would change when I was old enough to make it happen in whatever way it presented itself to me.

I have always paid attention to signs. Ever the observant kid, I paid attention to everything. I think this helped me survive. When a sign presented itself, I moved on it. Two of the signs were when my friend Jana came into my life, then a little later, my friend Cindy. Cindy was a neighbor I went to school with and she and I connected. She could see the gentle side of me and so did Jana. My sister was dating a boy who lived next door to us; he and I also became friends. I think he knew I needed a guy friend, so he befriended me. I will never forget these three people. They helped me find a glimmer of confidence in myself, and I made them new lights in my meadow. They were easy to talk with and were decent people. I didn't trust them right away—not until they showed me I could.

One of the things I noticed about them was they never talked about other people. They didn't gossip or judge. They showed me what a quality friendship was like and reinforced my ability to have quality people in my life. Even without being confident, they helped me cope. One of the first things they told me was that I should be glad I was not like my family or the people I thought I wanted to be friends with.

"You're a nice guy, Steve," they said. "You treat people decently even though you aren't being treated the same. Don't change."

It was wonderful, being seen and accepted for who I really was. I was not alone anymore. Being seen may be one of the most precious gifts a person can give to another. My gift was always leading with my smile, even though it wasn't always well received. I smiled through many tears and heartaches. It didn't work every time because there were people who tried to break me, but I was stronger, so they couldn't. My smile remains my trademark.

I wondered why anyone would want to take away someone's smile, to say or do something that would intentionally inflict pain. It was beyond my comprehension, but early on, I figured out people had issues. My issue appeared to be knowing I liked boys, and from my perspective, that didn't seem like much of an issue. I think a lot of people who gave me trouble were intimidated because of my integrity, confidence, and resolve. These are traits many of them didn't have, and I like to think I intimidated their insecurities. I was so far removed from them in this respect, they didn't know what to do with me. Without saying a word, just by my actions, by smiling and being kind, I was already ahead of them emotionally. Realizing this, and having formed trusting friendships, more confidence crept into my psyche.

I kept quiet about my friends, knowing if others found out, they would try to destroy the friendships. Little did I know, my friends understood this. Integrity issues were plentiful—then as now. Lies were created to make someone look bad and to bolster the weakness of those who wanted to look and feel better about themselves by diminishing others. Lies and psychological issues were rampant.

...riences informed me that almost everyone I knew had integrity ...nd major character flaws they used to try to keep people *in their* ...if someone stepped out of line, they were quickly put back in line— ...ie created to isolate and subdue those they saw as different. Learning this in pieces when I was younger, then later realizing that is how many of the people I was raised with thought and behaved, it helped me realize people in general build up their egos by manipulating the truth. While I was overwhelmed at first by rejection and abuse, it came to me after I left that I was fortunate to not be inflicted with such emotional dysfunction. I attribute my healthier psyche to leaving when I was nineteen to join the Air Force.

I found out early on that I opened myself up for battle by standing up for the right thing against people who didn't. I never understood why it was so hard for people to do the right thing. Maybe if men were raised to be in touch and honest with their feelings and emotions, instead of believing power came from starting and spreading lies, it would be a good thing. But it wasn't then and isn't now a prominent trait. There are still those who will continue to pick on others because their hearts are also beaten down.

Bottom line here is this: If people need to belittle someone else to bolster their own ego, they are not worth being around. It took time, patience, and *my lights* for me to learn I was different in a good way. I could stand on my own strengths, and I didn't want belittlers, betrayers, or abusers in my life— people who are followers and don't care about the truth, who are bullies with fake bravado.

My message here is simple: Be who you are, show your strength, and don't allow anyone to take that awareness or strength from you. I'm writing this as a mature adult, with my emotional intelligence intact. Having lived through this, I can see it everywhere. Some people can change, but most don't without some outside force holding up a mirror. Now I'm told that my confidence radiates, and those who want to be around me are equally confident and self-knowledgeable. I treat people the way I want to be treated, and I am proud of this.

It does hurt, knowing how much wasted time and emotions I spent dealing with trying to figure out why people were so cruel. But I did learn it, and this awareness has kept me being me and safe throughout my life. "I keep my distance from anyone who wants power over others. Shit—it's in politics, in the news, at every level of society and type of organization we are supposed to look up to and trust. In truth, they are only looking to be better than others in a world where honesty and virtues are severely lacking. I hold people accountable, which is why, to this day, I am an outcast in my family. I do know my strong integrity played a much larger role than being an outcast.

I regret all those years I believed I wasn't worthy of the goodness of life everyone else was experiencing because of who I was. It wasn't just because I was effeminate and emotional; I didn't know what made me different. My peers let me know I was queer. When I learned what I was, I thought I had kept that fact invisible, unaware my mannerisms and effeminate ways were visible to others. It seemed that everyone had it easier than I did. I was different, and no one let me forget that. Looking back, I am glad they didn't let me forget that. They were all straight, supposedly, with their own issues, but their issues weren't ostracized as mine were. I think people could also see in me my unwavering strength because I didn't conform to their misguided and unrealistic ideals of themselves, the lives they were living, what was being shown on TV and, later, the internet. I seemed to be able to see the reckless abandonment they all had for living and creating relationships based on talking about others to build bonds.

Just when I thought I could be my own person, life would knock me around. It was Saturday night of my senior year, and like always, there was a dance in Prairie du Rocher, the small town where we all grew up. I asked Mom if I could use the car to take a friend to a dance at the Legion Hall. Mom gave me permission. It was the first time I had asked to take the car with a passenger, anywhere.

Some people made fun of my driving. I was trying to concentrate and felt a sense of responsibility. Then I had an itch on my face, so instead of calmly scratching it, I slapped my face, thinking I shouldn't have my hands off the wheel too long. Word got out that I had "slapped myself" and soon family and friends joined in making fun of me. But that wasn't the worst of it. Someone had given one of my riders some beer, which he threw up in the back seat. I got in trouble for letting him drink even though I didn't know he had been and Mom made me clean up the car. Another time I felt being the oldest was used against me. I felt like I had been set up to fail.

8 : The Big Decision

I knew my inner strength wouldn't let me down. To survive, I had no choice.

Between my junior and senior year, I landed a part-time job working in the laundry of the hospital in Red Bud, not the same one as my grandmother worked in, but the new one they built. I only went to school in the afternoon my junior year, which was enough. I was quiet and tried not to attract attention. I even tried to suppress any coughs, so that when one broke loose, it sounded like I had imploded and was one hundred times worse than if I had just coughed. Everyone in the classroom looked at me in horror. I was scared to be looked at or noticed. Even having my name called out in class sent fear through me, as I always waited for the laughter or snickers to follow.

Thanking the Universe that I made it, my final year of school, I attended morning co-op classes to fulfill my remaining credits to graduate. I went to school for three hours starting at six a.m., then worked in the laundry after that for the rest of the day. I stayed under the radar and out of sight. I would come home, talk with my sister's boyfriend, Cindy, and Jana sometimes. I looked forward to talking with them. As I was nearing graduation, I was fearful of what to do when I graduated. I knew I didn't want to go to college and be subjected to more ridicule. I remember thinking I wanted to leave everything I'd known so that I could grow into who I was meant to be in the first place. I didn't know what that was, but I knew I had to make a change.

My senior year of high school was ending when the Universe came through for me again. I saw a military man walk out of the restroom. Although I was going in a different direction, something made me turn around and follow him. It was a chance meeting. If I had taken the hallway to the right, I would have missed him. I followed him to the counselor's office and asked if I could talk with him.

"Yes, come in." he said. "Have a seat. Are you interested in joining the Air Force?"

I told him truthfully, "I wasn't until I saw you walking in the hall." The thought of joining the military had never entered my mind—I mean, *the man's* military. I didn't see myself as a man. I was overwhelmed with the thought of it. I still didn't know what I was going to do. I only knew school was ending and I had to leave, that I couldn't stay in this area. I needed to develop who I knew I was away from everything and everyone I'd known. Plus, I wanted to make my parents proud of me.

"Why do you want to join?" he asked.

"I want to leave here and do something important with my life." I left out the real reasons. I didn't want to go to college. I couldn't stay around the people I grew up with. I was essentially joining the Air Force to save my life.

"Good," he said, then began to tell me all about the Air Force. "Do you have any family in the military?"

"My great uncle served in WWII in the Army Air Corps and my godfather, who is also an uncle, was in the Air Force in the sixties."

"Have you talked about this with either of them?"

"No, but their being in the Air Force was admirable to me." I looked up to both uncles. I saw my godfather all the time and knew he was a good man. I told my godfather after I signed the paperwork. My great uncle lived in Nevada, and I never got to see him, but my grandma told me what he had done and how proud he was to have been in the Air Force. When I called my great uncle, he said "Alright," then proceeded to tell me about the military, the education I would receive, and the adventures. "Most importantly," he added, "is serving and protecting this great nation so that the rights and freedoms we all enjoy are preserved and defended."

"I would like to join after I graduate," I told the recruiter.

He started the paperwork.

I told my friends Cindy and Jana about what I wanted to do. I had some doubt about my ability, but knew I had to do this. They encouraged me and supported me the entire time. I had some very long talks with each of them as to why I wanted to leave, and that I needed to do this to change my life. We talked about the dreams we had for ourselves and that the world held what we needed.

A few weeks went by, and the recruiter came back to the high school. By this time, I was almost through with school and graduation was around the corner. He brought paperwork to me to have my parents sign as I was still in high school.

Before I took the papers, the sergeant asked me two questions. "Do you smoke marijuana?

I said, "No." I didn't do drugs; I was afraid of them.

"Are you a homosexual?"

I thought it was odd but also knew the times dictated this question. "No," I answered. As far as being gay, I knew I was but was not going to have this stop me from living my potential and developing the strength I knew I had in me. I felt it was ignorant to hold someone back because of their sexuality. I wasn't going to let it prevent me from becoming who I knew I could be. I knew my potential and was determined to achieve it. I also knew I had to leave. I couldn't stay in the area where I grew up, where too many people saw me as worthless. That proverbial box was ever-present.

I took the paperwork home, surprising both Mom and Dad with the news of me joining. Shocked, Mom signed the paperwork right away; she knew I had to do this.

My dad was reluctant. "You can't join the man's military. You don't have it in you."

I said, "I do, Dad, and what I don't know, they will teach me. I don't want to be here anymore, and farming is not my life."

"You're telling me what I already know."

I wonder now if he was scared for me or felt he didn't do enough to help me grow into a man. He did everything he could. His knowledge and experience of raising a boy like me was severely limited.

Being headstrong about my life, I insisted this was what I wanted. He signed the paperwork and then walked out to the barn with his emotions. I never knew what he was feeling, but his head was down and he stayed in the barn for a good while. Maybe he was processing feelings of fear, regret, or pride. I knew I was doing what I had to do. That Monday, I took the paperwork back to the recruiter at the high school, turned it in, and was set to enter the military system after I graduated in May 1980.

Steve's senior picture, 1980.

The next step was to go through a series of physicals and tests at the Military Entrance Processing Station (MEPS) in St. Louis, Missouri. I passed everything and was put in the delayed enlistment program on September 11, 1980, which secured my slot for basic training in January 1981. This one decision changed my life forever. What it did was save my life.

I came back home and began telling more family and friends what I had done. No one believed I had joined the Air Force. Most everyone viewed me as a weak, inadequate, emotional person, lacking confidence. At first people thought I was lying about it. No one really took me seriously, except my mom and dad, as they'd signed the papers.

I spent the last few months working in the laundry at the hospital in Red Bud. These ladies and my bosses thought I was pretty cool. They saw me for who I was, a young boy who had a great smile, nice disposition, and was naive to the world. They loved me and supported me but also corrected me on things they thought weren't for me or some things I would say. Their perception wasn't skewed by gossip and disgust. The men and women I worked with weren't family or people I'd known at school; they were strangers who were older and wiser. Their opinions of me were different. I let my personality show with them. We had a good time working together, and to this day, I remember every single one of them. These people made me feel I was worthy and that I was viable as a young adult. The feelings of confidence I received and began to build on were spectacular. I looked forward to going into work every day. Being with them affirmed who I was and that I wasn't broken. They are all gone now, but I will never forget how they made me feel: confident, warm, and someone who mattered, was respected, and was loved and made a difference. These were deep, affirming feelings. I miss them and wish they could see the result of what their friendships and belief in me helped achieve. These people were also added as lights of mine. Most of these people were my grandparents' ages. They could see I was struggling, but instead of criticizing, they encouraged me to be the best I could be at my age. They also knew I would be leaving for the Air Force after the first of the year.

9 : Be Proud

The strength it took for me to join the Air Force was forged from desperation. It was mine alone. I didn't need approval. I just knew I had to do this. The trust I was supposed to have for my family had eroded. I didn't trust them because they kept showing me that I shouldn't. I give myself credit for seeing through the lies, half-truths, and their egos. I thought for myself and listened to my own instincts. This is one piece of me that I'm glad I have as a defense; it makes me step back and evaluate before I let anyone get close. It has served me well. I have people I look up to and admire, yet still, at times, I hold back. I second- and third-guessed myself, my feelings, and thoughts because something doesn't feel right. Instincts! My gut is usually right. I move on.

My dad put on a going-away party for me in Renault at the church hall. It was my siblings, a few friends, and my cousins. I had a date, but the girl was hanging out with another guy. This is the first time a close family member stood up for me and told her to, "Get back to Steven; he is your date tonight." The girl left with someone else. I had a nice time because I knew I was leaving. This little three-piece band played the Air Force song for me.

There was only a week or so left before I shipped out, and folks kept stopping by my mom's house to see me before I left. Wayne, the man Mom was dating at the time, demonstrated how to be confident and not let what people say bother me. This was nice, but until I could feel it within myself, the words were really lost on me. I had to feel I was worthy and feel my own confidence and happiness before anything could change in my psyche. He was a nice man, and I felt he looked out for me. We talked about his military days in Germany and when he was in the Army back in the 1960s during Vietnam. He shared a few of his struggles, which helped me know we all have struggles. He told me he was proud of the fact I was joining the military. He also knew I had to leave. He thought it would be the best thing for me. Both he and Mom talked with me and shared their opinions of how things wouldn't be the same once I leave. They said, "When you come back, everyone will still be doing the same things and living the same way, but you will have changed." They were both proud of me. I think my mom was even more proud because I had the guts to leave.

Wayne let me know he was proud of me and that I would make a great military man. I will never forget the conversations he and I had about that before I shipped out.

"Be proud of yourself," he said. "Not many people make a decision like this to change their lives. Only a few do, so be proud of that. You will be serving and protecting your mom, me, your family…everyone who is an American citizen. What could make you more proud? You are doing something for all of us to preserve and protect our freedoms. Just remember that. These young people who think they know it all don't know you. This time, I also felt some jealousy directed at me—unusual but still uncomfortable. You are doing something most of the people around here don't have the balls to do. Be proud of that." He was right.

I will never forget him or his words of encouragement. He believed in me and became one of my lights too. He is no longer with us, but he left an impression on me that I respect and remember. His words were given to me, no one else. This was another validation the Universe sent to me.

I had to pass a test to get into the Air Force, covering everything from mechanics to administration. I passed all of them and, based on my scores, was able to be placed in an administrative job. This proved to me that I was fairly smart. It was the first sign that I could hold my own with my book smarts. I was told the Air Force develops the mind, and I found it to be true. I was proud of that.

The day arrived for me to ship out. I can still hear the footsteps of my mom walking across the upstairs floor to wake me up. I hardly got any sleep because I was very anxious, thinking about leaving.

Mom called my name, in a sweet mom voice: "Steven, it's time to get up."

I went upstairs with my bag, waited for a few minutes until my brother and Wayne got ready, then I went to my other brother and my sister, who were still sleeping, to say goodbye. It was around four in the morning.

The last call I made was to my dad to let him know I was shipping out. He said to me, "You're in the man's military now. You are strong, do what they say, and be proud of yourself as we all are." His voice cracked, and I cried a little. That was the second time Dad ever said he was proud of me. I think he was a little scared for me. I was a little guy, picked on a lot, and didn't really have any kind of confidence. I doubted my ability, but I knew I had to do this to survive. Mom knew it too. Wayne, Mom, and my little brother took me to the Belleville MEPS to ship out. It was around five in the morning; ice and snow were falling. I was quiet, as were they. I'll never forget that day, saying goodbye to them. It was a somber moment. Wayne, Mom, and another family member hugged me and told me they loved me. The last thing Mom said, as her voice cracked, was she was proud of me too. No other words were spoken as the tears were at the ready. With tears in my eyes and my bag in hand, I made my way to the bus. I was scared. They watched me get on the bus that would take me to St. Louis to process out. Mom and Wayne knew I was about to embark on a journey that would change me forever, and it has. Mom told me some years later, she cried her eyes out as she watched me walk away, this little, skinny kid with a small bag, her son, leaving for the military. I wonder if she questioned whether she had done all she could do for me as my mother. That one decision was the single most important and best decision I have ever made for myself. When I left, I had no intention of coming back. I didn't talk about that, but that is what I was feeling. I wanted to leave all the people and backward-thinking ways. Finally, though, Mom and Dad were a light for me.

The bus took me to the MEPS in St. Louis to process out. It was a full day of tests, physicals, briefings, and a lot of waiting around. That night, we were paired up and assigned a roommate then taken to a hotel in downtown St. Louis. Even this experience was foreign to me. I had never stayed in any hotel, let alone a high-rise hotel in the middle of a big city. Neither my roommate nor I could sleep. We looked out of the fifteenth-floor window at the street life below us. It was amazing to watch and hear all the city noise. We finally went to bed, and morning came pretty quickly.

Dressed and ready, we were picked up by the bus again and taken back to the MEPS. After more processing, it was time to fly to San Antonio, Texas, for basic training. That flight to Texas was amazing to me, as I had never flown before. I was with guys on the plane, standing up and talking and laughing.

I remember thinking, *everyone is taking me for me, not a preconceived thought of what people back home thought of me*. My personality, what I managed to keep alive, was being noticed and was compatible to these strangers who were letting me know by their interactions that I was a decent person. They liked me. It was a comforting feeling. We landed in San Antonio and were escorted to a waiting bus to take us to Lackland AFB. I arrived shy, quiet, and scared. I knew my family and friends doubted that I would survive boot camp. For me, it was more of a mental challenge than physical. I was waiting to prove to myself and all the doubters that they were wrong.

We got off the bus, full of anticipation and anxiety, none of us knowing what was ahead. Immediately the Training Instructor (TI), a staff sergeant with a small mustache and stern eyes, stood with his hands behind his back and started yelling at us to get off the bus, line up, stand at attention (none of us knew what that was). He continued to yell. It was around 10 p.m. when we arrived. The TI told us to line up one behind the other, making four or five rows, so we did, all while the yelling continued as we didn't know what we were doing. After we were lined up, the TI said to "pick up your bags, drop your bags, who told you to pick them up?" It was like this for about five minutes. Surprisingly, though, I felt some confidence and self-esteem just by being in basic training, being present about the decision I made for myself.

Here I was being yelled at and belittled along with everyone else. I was proud of the fact I made this choice for no one other than myself. We were finally marched into the dorm, the 3702 Barracks. *Second to None* was our motto. We were assigned our bunks. It was a Friday night when we arrived, so we couldn't get uniforms or process in until Monday. We stayed in our civilian clothes to get our heads shaved and get briefings. When Monday came, we were finally issued uniforms, towels, underclothes, etc. We received all of our vaccines like we were on an assembly line. The first day was filled with all the in-processing we needed to do. Our civilian clothes were put in a locked room.

I had been in basic training for about two weeks when one day, after another briefing, my TI dismissed everyone but me. He walked up to me with his smokey bear hat bouncing off my forehead and said to me, "You're a fucking faggot, aren't you?"

I was scared but didn't let him know it. "Sir, no sir!" I answered.

He asked me again. I answered again, "Sir, no sir."

He said, "I think you are, and if I catch you looking at any of my men, I will have you kicked out of here so fast you won't know what hit you. I don't like faggots, and I will not have any in my flight. Have I made myself clear?"

Basic training picture,
February 1981.

I answered, "Sir, yes sir."

He then said, "You are dismissed."

I was shaken to the core with what had just taken place. I went back to my bunk, crawled under it like I was making my bed, and gathered my thoughts. Man, I was petrified, but I kept it together. I had to keep my strength and focus about me. The next day, we had our individual pictures taken for our professional Air Force picture, which was sent home to our families. In my photo, I have a stern expression. My eyes were off to the side, and I wasn't smiling. I was staring at my TI as he was telling the sergeant standing next to him, "This one here is my faggot I was telling you about." I could hear him saying it. Every time I look at my basic training picture, I hear his words. After the photo shoot, my bunkmate could tell I was flustered and asked what happened. I didn't tell him what really happened. I just said, "I need to do better."

I hardly slept thinking about what had taken place. I was terrified of being kicked out. I had no place to go. I joined the Air Force to save my life. I had to make this work. I couldn't go back home a failure, to all that backward, humiliating prejudice. I wouldn't have been able to survive that defeat. I had no place to go other than the military. So, I decided I had to get rid of whatever it was he was seeing in me. Any effeminate ways must go.

There was an Airman (Amn) who was flight chief in basic with the rest of us. A few years older than me, he was in charge of keeping an eye on all of us when the TI wasn't around. He was very masculine. As a point of interest, I didn't even have the need to shave yet. I was never taught how to do it. I had to learn how to do it in basic training. I thought, *I'm going to copy his movements and mannerisms to make them my own.* I watched how he stood to shave, took a pee, ate lunch, made his bed, took a shower, walked. I emulated everything he did so that my movements weren't so effeminate: the way he marched, stood to talk with someone, etc. I observed very discreetly, not wanting to bring attention to myself, staying true to my determined, focused mission. One night I was on dorm guard duty, standing at a post inside the hallway of the barracks guarding the door. We were not allowed to have anyone enter who could compromise the safety of the basic trainees sleeping. A sergeant came to the window and knocked on it loudly. He showed me a driver's license. It wasn't the proper form of military ID, and he wasn't in uniform.

I said, "Sir, you are not allowed to enter this area because you don't have proper identification."

He yelled and screamed at me, "I will have you court-martialed for not letting in a superior."

I said, "Sir, yes sir. Show me proper identification and I will let you in."

He yelled some more and left. I stared at him through the window, never wavering, following protocol. All through basic training, I perfected marching, sizing all my clothes in my closet, paying attention to every detail, and did very well. I only had one 341 pulled (these were demerits for things you do wrong and are kept folded under the flap of our breast pocket for easy access to be pulled). I was never recycled, which meant going backward and having to repeat a week's worth of training in another flight.

At the end of my training, upon graduation, that same TI came back to me and said, "You surprised me, Airman Zeiger. You graduated with honor and in good standing, and believe me, I was watching you the entire time. Congratulations! You earned your right to graduation from basic training and to be in the Air Force." I ended up graduating basic training in an Honor Flight.

 My confidence received an incredible boost. I knew without a doubt that my mind was more powerful than most people I knew. I survived basic training with honors. This was my first acknowledgment that I was worthy of bigger things, things which would demand me to be my best self and rise to every challenge. We were given a yearbook of sorts after graduation that detailed our flight history from beginning to end. Many of my fellow basic trainees signed my book and I signed theirs. It was the first time I felt accepted completely by my peer group as one of their equals. One note meant the most to me. The Airman wrote in my yearbook, "Ziggy, take it easy and good luck in the AF. You were one of my best men. Chief."

He had no idea how much that message meant to me or the impact he'd had on me from the beginning of basic. Reading that message as I was leaving basic created an indelible moment for me. The pride I felt accomplishing this without being recycled or having more than one 341 pulled was over-whelming. To this day, I can't express what this man meant to me. I got through basic training by shadowing and imitating him. I wish I could find him now to let him know how he helped me survive.

I only cried once in basic, and it was just a few tears. I received a Valentine's card from Mom. She and my sister wrote a message to me in the card that I still have: "We are proud of you and love you." Receiving these words from them made me emotional, as it affirmed to me that they did care.

I went to my bunk, laid under it where no one could see, and shed a tear or two. Under the bed was a good place because you could pretend you were tightening your bed to bounce a quarter, all the while hiding your emotions from others.

10 : My Mission: To Reconnect

Normal is an illusion.
What is normal for the spider is chaos for the fly.
~ Charles Addams, creator of the Addams Family

By the time basic training ended in March, I'd added a few more lights to my meadow. I had a follow-on assignment to be trained in my Air Force Specialty Code (AFSC), which was Administration Specialist 70230B. I was put on a bus then shipped out to Technical School at Biloxi AFB in Mississippi for six weeks.

It was cool. I had a good roommate. I went to class every day, made some friends, and hung out on the beach. This girl started to like me, so I would hang in the quad with her and a few new friends. She liked me, I liked her, but I knew it wouldn't go anywhere, even though I was being faced with my sexuality daily. I was strong and maintained myself.

I flew home once I graduated from Technical School. I distinctly remember landing in St. Louis and walking through the airport with my uniform on. I could see my family at the end of the arrivals gate waiting for me. I walked up to Mom and gave her a big hug, and she cried. All my siblings were there, including my sister's boyfriend, who was one of my lights. Wayne was there too. I was carrying my big drab-green duffel bag, and when we got to the car, I sat it down so that Wayne could open the trunk for me to put it in. Instead of me grabbing it, my sister's boyfriend did, but he struggled to lift it into the trunk. I took it from him and put it in the trunk easily. My mom later told my grandmother and her sisters, "You should have been there. The boyfriend struggled to pick up the duffel bag. Steven took it with ease and put it in the trunk. I was so proud as I could see Steven was already stronger and acted differently." It was a nice welcome home for me. When we were in the car, my brother said, "Steven sounds different." I remember thinking that he was hearing how I'd lowered my voice during my training to be like the chief.

For a day or two, it was nice being home. I went down to see Dad. When he saw me in my uniform, he started to cry and told me how proud of me he was. I think he knew I would be someone in spite of how I was treated at home. He definitely knew I was strong. We sat and talked for a while, then he took me over to Grandma and Grandpa's house where they got to see me too. I felt respect from Dad that I'd never felt from him before. I think that moment changed how my grandpa saw me too. He treated me differently after that, up until his death. My grandpa told me, after I joined the Air Force, how proud of me he was. When he saw me in my uniform, he cried with a lot of pride in his tears. I held my grandfather in high regard from then on. Every time I would come home on leave, I would make a visit to see him and my grandma. Our conversations were about what I was doing and where I was going and life events. He and Grandma would talk about the things going on in the family and their health. My relationship changed dramatically with him. I loved that and was so thankful I had a relationship with him.

It was nice being home, but I was ready to leave again after a few days, as the old prejudices started to creep in again. This time, I also felt some jealousy—unusual but still uncomfortable.

My first assignment was at Fairchild AFB in Spokane, Washington. I worked in an office that used keypunch cards to keep supply inventories. My supervisor was a staff sergeant. She seemed nice but really wasn't a good supervisor. She seemed to have emotional issues, but I didn't know enough about life to figure it out. It wasn't until a little later that I found out she didn't like me and transferred me downstairs to work for a staff sergeant. He was a good supervisor, and I learned a lot from him. I was there for about six months then was transferred over to the 92nd Bomb Wing's Orderly Room across the flight line to work.

By then, I'd made a friend who I fell in love with. He was straight
were (or at least, I thought they were). Anyway, I attached myself
he was close to me too. As our friendship grew, so did my feeli
He felt it too and didn't do anything to dissuade me from flirtin
wrestle, and so I would too, as I was getting the body contact
We fought a few times, just yelling at each other, and other people were
beginning to think we were in a relationship. That's when he started pulling
away. This emotional upheaval started to affect my work, and I was nearly
kicked out of the Air Force because of it. Emotional problems developed
because I'd never experienced liking someone on this level before. It affected
my job performance. All I wanted to do was be with him, even though he
didn't feel the same.

I was in a lot of trouble, so I decided to see a counselor to talk about everything, except sexual feelings, which I couldn't reveal. Even though I couldn't
reveal my love for him, it helped to talk about being rejected by a friend.

The counselor asked, "Do you know who you are?"

My reply was honest. "I think I do, but I lose sight of me all the time." She
suggested I take some leave and go home to figure some stuff out.

My former supervisor, the staff sergeant, went to bat for me and saved my
career. He told the squadron commander that "Amn Zeiger is a good soldier.
He needs firm guidance and training, and I don't think he is receiving it."
After a few hours of deliberating on my being kicked out, the staff sergeant
took me back to his office. "The commander assigned me to be your supervisor." He said, "I will train you and you will learn. My name is on the line
with the commander."

I understood it at the deepest level of survival. I shared with him my
emotional issues growing up and how they affected my confidence. After
working with that staff sergeant for a very short time, I focused on my strong
work ethic and got back to where it needed to be. Then the staff sergeant
agreed it was time for me to take some leave and go home.

Going home felt like a mission to reconnect with myself. I started by bringing
back my beautiful character, virtues, and heart, endowing each with strength.
Returning to the place I grew up, I interviewed people who had known me

as a kid, the ones I trusted to tell me the truth about the kind of kid I was. I needed to validate in my mind who I truly was. Those years of hiding huge parts of me, watching them float away, proved to be pieces that made me, me, I was missing me and needed to find myself. Emotionally lost but with renewed strength, I pieced together the parts I was struggling with that I needed to understand to regain confidence in myself. I still had a long way to go to really understand who "Steve" was, but I was exploring my thoughts and feelings so I could survive.

When I returned to Fairchild, I worked long, hard hours for the same staff sergeant. I put together our 92nd Bombardment Wing Maintenance Standardization and Evaluation Program Report each quarter. This report was about sixty pages of dialogue, numbers, and stats—everything that had to do with our wing. The information contained had to be 100 percent correct because this report was given to the commander for his update of the progress of the Wing. Every member of the Quality Control office gave me their written inputs to include in this huge report. I was given an award for the professionalism, accuracy, and timely manner in which I completed it. I had completed it ahead of schedule each time. I took responsibility for myself and the products I produced.

I felt pride and confidence building, and I knew my potential was being elevated. My staff sergeant made the time to train me to be the best Air Force Airman I could possibly be. It was like a dream come true for my mental well-being. It provided another example of how, when I put my mind to it, I could make changes. I stayed in, the discharge paperwork was thrown away, and I flourished.

Some of the family flew out to Spokane to visit me. I was surprised they wanted to come out to do that. I took them around the base, and they met the staff sergeant. We toured Spokane. It was a nice visit for them and for me.

I became good friends with the staff sergeant and his wife. He asked me to be the godfather to their only son. Later in life, he passed away from cancer. I flew down to Texas for his funeral and gave his eulogy. This was hard for me to deliver because of what this man meant to me. I haven't stayed in touch with the family, but I think of them often. I will never forget what that staff sergeant did to save me and my career.

11 : My Faith System

Why would I believe in something that saw me as damaged? How can people say they are faithful and still treat others badly? The message to me was they didn't believe it either.

Being raised Catholic then being confirmed and becoming part of the Catholic Youth Organization (CYO) was all lost on me. I didn't believe it, for one; second, most people I was being raised with never used any of the principles that I could see about being good people—at least, not based on how they treated me. Third, I once asked the priest about the Bible.

"If the Bible was created from the beginning of time, with Adam and Eve in the Garden of Eden, and it took seven days to create the earth, stars, and everything on the planet, why aren't the dinosaurs mentioned in it?" I asked.

He was offended, and I stopped going to CYO, which Mom wasn't happy about. However, Dad looked at me with sort of a smile. I think he liked that I was thinking for myself. Dinosaur remains weren't discovered until much later in the human timeline, certainly not before the Bible was written. Archaeology wasn't a concept yet. In my opinion, I see the Bible as a man-made book to control the masses—that's all. I needed some sort of faith to believe in and knew there was a higher power out there, just from my own intellect. I started exploring other faiths but ultimately couldn't believe in any organized religion.

I was and am an independent thinker. I don't believe the choice of a religion should be mandated for a baby or child. This is a choice they should make for themselves as they get older and start understanding the Universe as they see it. My experience of religion is that it is designed to make you either hate yourself or others, or both. It is designed to divide.

I had to learn to love myself despite my socialization and school prejudice and the added pressure of a religion that supported my community and those people who shared these beliefs. I knew it didn't support me. It was incredibly eye-opening to see these people treat me the way they did and then go to church and worship their goodness.

I've learned you have to love yourself, and eventually, you'll love others. The love you have for yourself is the most important love one can have. Loving others comes from that.

I didn't respect what some of my family and community believed because they don't live how God professes they should, with love, compassion, acceptance, etc.

A church created to control the masses (my belief) that made being gay offensive was based on money too. Because, in those days, gay people didn't spend money in the church to get married or have kids to get baptized because the church made it a sin. Many lives were ruined because gays and lesbians tried to fit into that dogma of thinking.

For me, it seems too many people are treated badly for nothing. What gives people the right to tell or make others feel bad about who they are or tell them what they should believe? My faith system is completely different and serves me well. It's an intimate relationship I have with myself and that realm in the Universe. I discovered I have a significant amount of Viking DNA running through my veins from a home DNA test I took. I now follow those beliefs.

12 : The Passing of My Dad

You can't take a set of car keys, a wallet, or your flat screen with you. You only take what's in your heart when it is time for you to pass over. This is where value should be placed.

A little over a year after I joined the military, my dad was diagnosed with cancer of the liver. I was notified by the Red Cross that he was in the hospital with not much time to live. He was in and out of the hospital from this point on, and finally, it was time for the hospital to make a decision. There wasn't anything else they could do for him. The hospital staff talked with his parents about taking him home to live out his remaining days.

On a Sunday morning in May, I was on leave to be with Dad and visit him at my grandparents' house. My sister, Little Mary, my friend from the military, and I were in the kitchen. Dad was sitting on the bench swing outside under the tree, and he motioned for someone to come out to him. My sister ran out there then came back in and said, "Steven, Dad wants to talk with you."

I went out to him, sat on the bench swing next to him, and I asked, "How are you doing?"

At this point, his speech was incredibly labored as a growth was growing into his voice box, but he was able to talk with me. Slowly, he told me, "Steven, I'm not going to be here much longer."

I said, "Oh Dad, you're strong. You can beat this."

He put his hand on my left leg and squeezed it and said, "No, I'm not." Then he said, "I always knew you would be the one to leave here. I knew you wouldn't stay around here."

That got my attention, and the air changed around us. I listened to him with so much intensity because there was a sincere seriousness to him, something that I haven't felt from anyone before or since.

He went on to say, "You are stronger than the rest. I see it, and I see that you are not afraid of living. I am not going to be here to guide the other three. You are going to have to be strong for your family; they aren't strong like you."

I knew he meant emotionally, not physically. I said, "Dad, they don't listen to me now and don't respect me."

"You will have to make them. I know you are different from the rest of the boys, and I know you know what I'm talking about. You will have it rough in life because of who you are. I want you to remember that when I'm not here, you will always carry my first name and my last name. These will give you the strength to get through any of the struggles life gives you."

In essence, he was telling me he knew I was gay. With this admission, I grabbed his hand as tears flowed down my cheek.

"I'm sorry," he continued, "for my actions that made your mom divorce me. I'd changed, and so had your mom."

I understood. Dad wasn't a hugger, and I wasn't at that time, so I held his hand as we looked at the bluff in front of us in silence.

"I will do my best," I promised him. He looked at me, nodded his head, then we both sat there looking at that beautiful blue sky above the bluffs, a slight wind moving green trees adorning the bluff. The puffy white clouds hung in that blue sky, cementing themselves in the picture that forever marked my time with my dad on that bench swing, making it feel everlasting. I think he wanted to make sure I knew what he wanted me to know; I remember every detail of that moment.

My brother and his then wife had a baby and named me her godfather. That was a major change in how my brother saw me. My niece was the only grandchild my dad got to meet.

My leave was ending the next day. I flew back to Fairchild AFB anticipating a call from Mom. Almost a month later, I got the call Dad had passed. I flew back home for his funeral. I will always have his validation, that moment when he told me how proud he was of me.

Little Mary remembers when this happened. She was watching out the window. Before Dad had passed, he and Mom reconciled, and there was forgiveness from both. I think Dad found peace with this and died shortly thereafter. I hated that this very proud, strong man with a generous heart was consumed by this dreadful disease. He will always be a strong man in my mind. He was my dad.

I returned to Fairchild AFB with a strong desire to explore a new place. I could do this in the military, and a few months after I returned to Fairchild, I received orders to Ramstein Air Base (AB) in Germany. I'd applied for this assignment a year earlier on my Dream Sheet—a form where you list different countries or states where you wish to be stationed. My orders came in, and I was assigned to the 322 Airlift Division at Ramstein AB.

I'd been friends with a man for more than two and a half years. We were heading emotionally, as well as physically, in different directions. The fact that I had a crush on him took its toll on our friendship. With the passing of my dad, strong emotions consumed me. He could feel what I was projecting. Our friendship broke down.

With the ruptured friendship and pain that resulted, I was ready to leave. But I wanted to remain friends and thought I would let him know how I truly felt about him. In my mind, I thought he would like to hear how he impacted my confidence and that I had a crush on him and loved him. It was a Friday night, and we were both in the apartment. I was preparing to get things in order to be shipped out. I thought it was a good time to sit down and have a nice talk with him. I let him know how I felt and what he meant to me. He stood up, punched me in the face, and proceeded to beat me up. I had black and blue eyes, a bloody mouth and nose. I was knocked out for a few minutes. As I was coming to, I saw him grabbing his coat and leaving the apartment. After he was gone, I got up and put ice on my face. I hoped the bruises would be gone by Monday. They weren't.

My supervisor and the Wing Commander's secretary, who happened to be my boss's mother, were in shock when they saw me. They were so concerned and wanted to know who had done this. I couldn't tell them who or why because I would have for sure been dishonorably discharged and also put my friend in some major trouble. With the staff sergeant putting his name on the line to keep me in the Air Force and all he had done for me the past year and a half, not to mention my personal growth, I didn't want to disgrace him by telling the truth about what had happened. So, I brushed it under the carpet and said I had gotten into a fight over a girl. Again, another lie. I realized, in retrospect, that I was severely upset by the passing of my dad and my emotions fueled my actions. Another lesson learned.

My final performance report [the Airman Performance Report (APR)] was written by my supervisor and then given to higher-ranking levels of sergeants and officers to add their comments about my performance. I was given a great review, which acknowledged my growth potential, and I was promoted to my next rank.

Before leaving for Germany, I flew home for a few weeks. I stayed to myself and saw a few family members before I left. I sensed my family felt the same about me. I told my siblings what my dad and I had talked about. They immediately told me I was lying about all of it. I wasn't surprised, but I held out hope they would receive it genuinely. They made it easy for me to leave. Heading for Europe, I said my goodbyes, knowing I would probably not be home during my time in Germany. I wanted to travel and see as many countries as I could. We only earned thirty days of leave a year, and I wanted to save mine to explore and travel. Especially since being home was among my least favorite places, and now that I was an adult with my own life, I didn't feel homesick. I looked at being home as going backward in my growth. At this time, I didn't know if I would ever return.

I was extremely excited about heading to Germany. I was assigned to the 322ALD for a few months then was reassigned to the 316 Supply Squadron, where I eventually became the noncommissioned officer in charge (NCOIC) of their administration office. I had just been promoted to sergeant. This was a great assignment for me. I was keenly aware of being in Germany. I'd made a few decent friends who were fun. They were people I trusted. I felt confident, my personality was standing on its own, and people saw me for who I was—a nice guy.

Since I was a sergeant now, I had the option of living off base. At that time, we were given an allowance in our pay to live out of the barracks. I jumped at that option and moved to Miesenbach, a little town not far from the base. I rode my bike to and from work every day.

It was the eighties! Everything was being invented or reinvented. I embraced the newness of the decade completely. I loved being stationed at Ramstein AB and loved my assignment. It was amazing being in a different country, experiencing a whole new culture. I finally had the independence I had been seeking my whole life. I felt I was being embraced fully and enjoyed being free. It was a powerful feeling. It felt like nothing could hold me back. The counseling I went through at Fairchild helped me move past a lot of my insecurity. I was interested in things I had never dreamed of trying, like snow skiing. I learned how to ski in the Alps of Switzerland. I went to many historical sites in France, Germany, Austria, and any country I could get to by train. I just enjoyed being in different countries, exploring. I was on my own for some of these travels, with friends on others. The feeling of empowerment started to build in me. I was on the world stage alone, living on my terms, experiencing life in a huge way. The early 1980s were a great time to be alive. It was the time of cell phones and computers, new age music and special-effects movies. The lifestyles of that decade were blowing the doors off mainstream society.

I was aware that my generation was pushing this, that I was part of a wonderful time with wonderful people. We were a lot more carefree than previous generations. Our political agenda was less intense. There weren't any wars to define us, so we were allowed to be freer with our self-expression and sexuality. We all embraced this carefree life.

Being in Europe during this time was unbelievably exciting. I got my ear pierced and had my first sexual experience with another man. I had a crush on this guy who was in my squadron. He was a year younger than I was, and we saw each other every day. We knew each other well enough that he asked me if I wanted to get a beer at a local Gasthaus. I said sure. We talked and laughed about stuff and got to know each other even better. When we were getting ready to leave, I asked him if he wanted to see where I lived. He said sure. He followed me to my apartment. I could tell he liked me. I was very nervous as I didn't know if he was undercover or not. I let him make the first move. This was in 1985. This sort of thing was not discussed, and people in the Office of Special Investigation (OSI) were looking for people who were gay, did drugs, or did other things considered illicit at the time to catch them in the act. I mean, we could have been dishonorably discharged. I was keenly protective of my military service and not harming it, but my sexual growth and desires were growing so strong, I couldn't hold them back. In the conversation, we asked each other if either of us was part of the OSI. We both assured each other that we weren't. We kissed in my living room. I can tell you, I felt like flying. I had so much feeling in me about the passion I felt. It was so strong I couldn't speak. For the first time in my life, I was able to show someone who felt the same as I did that I could be special to them and celebrate that specialness by being me. I could have floated around the room, buoyed by the acceptance I felt in myself.

He and I were together for the duration of my assignment, our kiss having progressed to intimate sexual relations. My world opened up, and "off came the doors of my closet." He showed me how to love and be loved by another man. He had much more experience than me, as I'd had none until him. We ended our relationship as I received orders to leave. I wasn't as heartbroken as I anticipated because I accepted the fact that I was leaving. My previous counseling helped me to realize some things "are just the way they are." I look back on this assignment and our relationship with fond, warm, loving memories. It meant a great deal to me to be on the world stage in Europe. That time is set apart in my memory forever. The '80s in general stir a heartfelt longing in my soul. I go to music and all things '80s when I want to relax and reflect on a beautiful time in my life.

A German lady who cleaned our office said to me, "You are so young looking. The genes you have will serve you well as you age." They have. I still don't look my age. She sent me on my way with this compliment.

After my assignment at Ramstein, I was stationed at Scott AFB in Illinois. I thought at the time it was a good thing because the base was an hour from my hometown. I thought it would be nice to see if my family had grown emotionally. I wanted them to experience me as a military man and share all the growth I had achieved up to this point.

Assigned to the 375th Maintenance Squadron, I was in charge of another office. I really enjoyed my job, had a renewed sense of self-confidence, and finally experienced my self-acknowledged sexuality. I was beginning to have crushes on all sorts of guys in my units. I kept it under wraps, as I didn't want anyone to know. I was also twenty-five and full of hormones. It wasn't easy, but I stayed in the closet and wasn't out to anyone. A few guys I tried to approach got turned off. It scared me so I didn't try anymore. The freedom and assurance I felt in Germany was not natural here. My emotions and feelings were mixed up, and I couldn't act on my nature.

I was maintaining my job performance, doing great things, but staying under the radar. Even though there were times I suffered from emotional issues and lacked confidence in my ideals, I kept growing, but I felt fake because I couldn't truly be me. I was lying to my family and pretty much everyone I knew about why I wasn't dating or doing what they considered normal to them.

With people I knew and grew up with being close by, I would visit and, with each visit, re-encounter all the old biases. It didn't matter that I was in the military. Comments like, "How the hell can the military operate with people like Steven in it?" By this time, it was clear to me that these insecurities and jealousies were not just with me, but for anyone who was not like them.

Another family member was getting married and was flying to out west for the ceremony. Other family members were invited. I wasn't because I was told I was an embarrassment. I brought a date (a girl) with me to the reception to be accepted. Doing that felt so weird. It wasn't me.

The traits I hid for so long were no longer hidden, so everyone was experiencing the real me. Yet, my sensitivity, emotional side, and thoughtfulness were seen as weaknesses. But there were contradictions, like the time I was asked to be the godfather to the newborn of one of my siblings. I think their spouse drove that decision.

Although I felt judged, people were noticing I was the kind of person who would take responsibility for both of the nieces for whom I was named godfather, one from each of my brothers. It was a weird dichotomy. It created conflict within me because they treated me poorly, yet I was trusted enough to be named godfather to their kids. They knew I was a responsible adult.

When I was stationed at Scott AFB, I rented a place in O'Fallon, Illinois, close to the base. It was a nice place, far enough away from my family but close enough to still be able to drive home. It was a perfect location for me. The apartment was actually a two-bedroom townhouse, as I wanted to get a roommate to share expenses. There was a pool on the property between all the apartment buildings where everyone would hang out in the summertime, listen to cool '80s music, and sometimes have drinks. It was great.

That's where I met my friend Pennie. We became instant friends and are friends to this day. One day Pennie actually pointed at a girl and said, "I think that girl likes you."

I asked, "How do you know?"

"She keeps staring at you."

I didn't think anything of it until she came over and started talking with me. I was taken aback. I had never had a girl come on to me like that before, even though I'd been told I was good-looking. We talked and started hanging out, even though I knew who I was and who I wanted. But since my friends were all getting married and starting families, I thought, "Why not? It will help with my image."

This is not me being flippant. I was still struggling with self-image, emotions, and insecurity issues. I started dating a young woman. I really liked her. Her personality complemented mine very well. She was instantly drawn to me and fell in love quickly. She was a beautiful Hispanic girl with long, wavy black hair and big brown eyes, a little shorter than me, and a smile that would stop a train with its beauty. She was full of life and creativity. She was an artist and could draw and paint beautifully. When she wrote letters to me, her words were descriptive and arranged in a way that can only be described as lyrics. I still have envelopes where she drew my face on the outside of them in pencil. My mailman said to me when he delivered my letters, "I knew this was for you when I saw it," and laughed.

She fell deeply in love with me. I started feeling love for her too but knew I couldn't sustain it and didn't want to hurt her down the road. I couldn't bear not being honest with her. We dated for about a year. We never had sex, and she thought it was because I respected her. We kissed a lot. I sort of used her to cover for me. If I'd been straight, I would have married her and lived happily. She was such a beautiful woman, inside and out. I ended up breaking up with her because I knew it wouldn't go anywhere. I broke her heart. To this day, I have all the letters she has written to me. I have never forgotten her. About fifteen years ago, I reached out to try to find her, which I did. I called to talk with her about that time and to apologize to her for hurting her. I told her I was gay, and I felt it wasn't fair to keep leading her on. I couldn't talk about it at that time because I was in the military.

She listened and said, "Thank you for telling me this. I always thought it was something I did."

I said, "No, it was me."

We both agreed the breakup was for the best. She felt so much better about herself after I told her about myself. I felt good about that too.

She said, "I'm not telling my husband about you being gay because sometimes I use you to make him jealous."

I laughed. "I don't mind that."

"You were the love of my life," she said.

It made me happy to hear this as I had never had an impact like that on anyone.

As an aside, I'd begun modeling in Germany and continued in Illinois. Coming from attractive parents, I had classic good looks for modeling. My mom and dad could both have been models, and it was something I'd always been interested in doing. I did print ads and other modeling, which the agency arranged. This boosted my confidence, especially after being told I was ugly when I was growing up. I finally knew, I was not an ugly guy.

Steve Zeiger of O'Fallon is wearing a splashy multicolored, handknit acrylic sweater by Cellini, $55, with a bright red cotton Hunting Horn shirt, $24.50 and black pleated corduroy trousers, $27.50, all from J. Riggings. Cindy Altschuh of Cahokia is wearing a black, jewel incrusted cardigan sweater by The Limited, $98, over

Credits
FASHIONS: J. Riggings and The Limited of St. Clair Square in Fairview Heights. STORY: Jim Haverstick of the Journal staff
PHOTOS: T. L. Witt of the Journal staff

Newspaper print ad featuring Steve and another model in sweaters.

13 : Leadership

**Leading means doing the right things,
and managing means doing things right.**

~ Warren Bennis

I was still working as the Noncommissioned Officer in Charge (NCOIC) of the maintenance orderly room and had two people under me. I always knew I had a natural leadership quality but, until now, had had little opportunity to experience it. As a sergeant, I started supervising people of lower rank.

My innate skills as a leader enabled me to be confident and assertive. I was never aggressive but led with an understanding of where people were in their development and respected it. I helped others grow into young leaders themselves. I became a mentor to quite a few people.

Having always had this ability but rarely allowed to act on it growing up, I relished earning this opportunity. The strange thing is this: growing up, if I asserted myself, I was put down and verbally belittled because people thought I was acting superior. I'm grateful the military celebrates strong leaders, enabling me to flourish and grow. I recognized the different levels of my AFSC, so I wanted to learn the other aspects of it. The administrative side of my AFSC was nice, but to grow, I felt I needed to explore other opportunities, thinking it would help me get promoted. I asked for and was granted a transfer to the Post Office. I learned this job quickly and found myself quickly bored, even though I'd gained additional knowledge. I knew that if an organization had a vacancy for an administrative person, they would contact the Post Office, where there was always personnel that could fill the requirement. As fate would have it, the Post Office was contacted by the 1361st Audiovisual Squadron needing another administrative sergeant. They contacted the Post Office to see if anyone would like to run their admin office, and my boss said, "We do—Sgt. Zeiger. He is more than capable to run your office and is a strong leader in the sense he will do what's right for the Air Force."

I was transferred over to the 1361st Audiovisual Squadron at Scott AFB the next day. This assignment was one of my best, as the commander took me under his wing and really supported me. My supervisor was a wonderful woman. Between her support and that of the colonel, my confidence soared, as did my performance. They believed in me. My supervisor trusted me to make the right decisions and also knew that if I made a decision that wasn't right, I would hold myself accountable for it. We had a wonderful working relationship. This was true for everyone in that squadron. Military and civilians alike, all the people who worked in the squadron, became my friends. I was allowed to be creative and embrace things that meant a great deal to me, as long as it supported the squadron. I started a recycling program, which the base eventually adopted. My commander was happy I did that and so were the squadron personnel. This was in 1989. At the end of each week, I would take all the tall trash cans, empty their contents into their separate bags, and take it down to a place that would discard it in the closest city to be recycled.

His commander suggested Steve get a professional picture taken as a sergeant.

Those days provided ample opportunity for me to grow, stretch, and take on new leadership roles. I was feeling good about myself and my capabilities. My leadership style felt very natural. I was respected and my input was welcomed. It was a powerful time for me. I'm glad my commander asked me to get professional pictures taken in my uniform. He told me that I should have them for promotion reasons and also for my family. I still have those pictures to remind me of that time and place in my life.

It was time again for me to reenlist, and my commander arranged for the commander of the Thunderbirds—fighter jets who performed in formation at the Scott AFB Air Show—to enlist me along with a few other service members. I have a picture of him, along with all the pilots of the Thunderbirds and a lithograph of each pilot signing their name on their respective jet.

Steve, second from left, is reenlisted, along with other service members, by the commander of the Thunderbirds.

My commander also decided it would be a great idea to drive to Red Bud, my hometown, to reenlist me in front of my mom and family members, so we did. Grandma and Grandpa were there along with my sister and a few others. My grandpa shed tears as I reenlisted. It was a proud moment for both of us. Grandpa, Grandma, Mom, and my sister had never seen something like it. It was a very proud moment, not just for me, but for my family.

Mom was beaming with pride. Grandpa told me, "Your dad would be very proud of you."

It was time again to get orders. I received my Enlisted Performance Report (EPR). These forms had changed by this time, but again, my reviews were outstanding. This is the first time my commander coined a defining phrase for me. He said I have "a quiet confidence" going on about me and that it served me well. I knew this was what I had in me, but having it recognized on a military platform was incredibly satisfying.

Steve, full of confidence, sitting at his desk, 1989.

I was sad to be leaving the squadron I was assigned, but I knew I had to. I volunteered to take a remote assignment to Keflavik, Iceland, which I thought would be beneficial, as I needed to study to make my next rank. I was assigned to the 57th Fighter Interceptor Squadron (FIS). My office was across the flight line, and there was only one other airman working there. I would be his supervisor. This young airman was smart, and as our working relationship grew strong, so did our friendship. He had a girl in the States and would talk about her and their plans to marry when he got back. He worked hard and was a decent young guy.

I also met Jane, who worked directly for the pilots. We became friends too. The difference between making friends at a remote assignment versus nonremote is the relationships seem to be that much tighter, as we are all together all the time. There wasn't any other place to go except the base, which had limited access, so the bonds were strong. In general, the bonds made with our military brothers and sisters are long-lasting. We respect each other. Anyone outside the military cannot understand. The nature of what we are all doing collectively as members of the military, and the oaths we all take to serve and protect, creates a powerful bond.

I was in the squadron for about a week when another member of the squadron came into my office. Our eyes locked. I knew right away that there was something different about him. He would come to my office and start chatting with me. I thought, "What a nice guy." Little did I know I would fall in love with him, and he with me. A rodeo performer, he was from Colorado Springs, Colorado, and was as beautiful as an Adonis to me. He could sweet-talk the sweetness right out of a piece of candy.

We lived in the same barracks, so at the end of the day, he would come up to my room and we would talk more. There were two bars on Keflavik: one was for rock and roll, the other for country. The Air Force guys didn't go to the rock and roll bar because that's where the Army, Marines, and Navy hung out and there were always fights. The Air Force personnel were not about that and didn't want to be part of it. That's when I learned how to line dance because all we had for entertainment was country music—not to mention, this guy that I was getting to know was a line dancer. It wasn't long before my line dancing skills were honed, as every weekend we would head over to the Windbreaker to drink and dance.

One night, he wanted to stay in the barracks, so I went down to his room to hang out. He handed me a Coors Light and said, "Steve, I want to talk with you about something."

Unbeknownst to me, he had this planned for about a week to make sure he had me pegged.

I said, "OK."

He beat around the bush a little then finally said, "I think you are like me."

I asked, "What do you mean?"

"You don't know?"

"Are you referring to me liking line dancing?"

He said, "No. I like you."

I said, "I like you too."

My hand was on the table. He grabbed my little finger, squeezed it, and said, "No, I LIKE you."

I got it. I was like, wow. "I like you too." That moment is etched in my memory. A feeling of exhilaration rushed over my body, tingling and new. I wanted to hold him and be held by him, to be intimate. The moment was more real than what I'd previously experienced because this was more meaningful. We were both in our late twenties and knew this wasn't an infatuation. These were true feelings.

Before this, I was experimenting, going with the hormones. I had never felt desired or loved in this way. It was like he and I were the only ones on the planet. He leaned over the table and kissed me. This was the second guy to ever kiss me. We made out with each other on his bed. It was the most beautiful thing I had ever done. I liked him a lot, and we bonded with each other. Our feelings for each other were intense, creating a mutual embrace of attraction and love.

He was cute and had a nice body. He had an open personality, was easy to talk with, was a great dancer, and was very charming in a cowboy sort of way. He was affectionate, carefree, and a lover of life. I can still see his eyes that made me feel wanted when he would look at me. His persona was that of a sexy man, with a warmth about him. We fell in love with each other. I knew it, and I could feel it through his eyes. He told me how he saw me and how he loved me. As fate would have it, his roommate transferred so he had space for a new roommate. We were very intimate with each other by this time, and about a week later, I changed rooms to live in his room. It was magical. It was the first time I felt like I was in a real relationship. For six months, we dated in his room; outside of it, we were just buds. Then the day came for him to ship out to his next assignment. On Keflavik, as with other remote assignments, the tours are only one year long. The movers came and packed up all his belongings, and a few weeks later, he shipped out. Before he left, though, he arranged for us to have a date night in his room. We didn't go to the Windbreaker to dance like we normally would on a Friday night. He created a space for us to be with each other privately. Naturally, the other guys came knocking on our door to see where we were because everyone was partying at the club. We acted like we weren't in there, but the knocking became worse as they suspected we were in there. I quickly got dressed, jumped out of our first-floor window, and ran to the other end of the barracks and came in the door. I acted like I had just come back from the club looking for them. It was a close call, for sure.

I was at work when he flew back to the States. When I came back to the barracks, I entered an empty room except for the letter he left for me on the table. When I saw it, I got emotional. I was missing him and what we had. I couldn't bring myself to read that letter for a few days. When I did, I wept for him. This was the first time I felt passionate love for someone. I missed him with all my being. What I felt from him and what I felt in myself for me was indescribable—sad beyond belief. He was the first love in my life, which made his leaving that much more painful. I was on this island and couldn't drive away or escape to process this. I stayed in that room and processed the loss the best I could.

He called me on our hall phone a few weeks later. "I'm safe in Texas."

"I miss you."

"I have to end our relationship. I met someone else."

Shocked, hurt, and angry, I said, "I don't want to talk to you again." Devastated and heartbroken, my issues of insecurity resurfaced. Later I realized that it had to be this way. I was not where he was, and I had a follow-on to Germany. I think people sensed we'd had a relationship. There was an incident at the Windbreaker when this brute of a guy grabbed me and threw me against the wall.

He said, "I think you're a fag."

I said, "Get the fuck away from me." He and I were the same rank. He took his hands off me, we stared at each other, and that was that.

14 : Out of the Military

I'd learned the importance of staying true to who you are, to being aware of your surroundings and paying attention to opportunities as they present themselves to you. Allow your heart to recognize what is meant for you, then just act on it. Take risks—that's the best part of living. Seek out what works for you and do not settle for what others think is best for you. To me, that is not living a quality life.

I ended up not making my next rank, as I didn't score high enough. As a result, I got word that the Air Force was downsizing, and I was one of thousands on that list. I flew back to McGuire AFB in New Jersey for processing out of the military. It seemed surreal to me to not be part of the military anymore. It had given me what I'd needed for my mental and emotional growth. I'd developed solid confidence in myself just from being part of it.

The thoughts I had as a kid growing up were true. I had grown into my potential. Now, there was so much more to develop as my future unfolded. My intelligence and creativity were growing along with all other aspects of my being. I allowed myself to take risks and make decisions based on the direction I wanted to go. Whatever decision I made, I made it work for me.

I don't necessarily believe in making a "wrong" decision. You make a decision, and then if it works, it works; if not, it was a lesson learned. I gained the experience and knowledge of myself to be all I wanted to be. I returned to Mom's house in Red Bud briefly. The old attitudes were the same as before I went into the Air Force. I had changed a great deal, but they hadn't. It was impossible for me to be around all that. I knew without a doubt that I was gay. I didn't want to be in Red Bud, so I headed for the city of St. Louis to explore its diversity and opportunities.

When I got off of active duty, I came out. I was turning thirty, so I had a party and invited some family members who I thought would attend. There were a few lesbians there, and of course, a few people I knew made a nasty joke about lesbians.

"That's enough," I said. "If you make fun of them, you make fun of me." My voice was stronger from all my experience now. I came out to them right there. They were uncomfortable and ended up leaving.

Before my sister left, she walked over to me in a protective manner, put her arms around my waist so all could see, and said, "I don't want you out in bars like that. It scares me."

I'll never forget that birthday. I was tired of constantly lying to people about my life. I knew I was a good guy, with lots of love and understanding. I never went back into the closet. No one is worth that. Lying hurt me worse than facing the reality. For about a year, my mom and brothers were distant; we talked very little and said nothing of importance.

My sister told me, "You should have just come out to me. I don't care if you're gay. I sort of knew it." She handled it better than the rest and took it upon herself to help them understand and accept me being gay. I applauded her efforts, but it didn't work all that well. This is when my relationship with my sister changed for the better. By her actions, she proved to me I was more than just her gay brother. I represented a freedom of sorts for her. She confided in me, and we remained close.

This set me free to live my next chapters, unencumbered by deceit and lies. I knew I had a good set of virtues and morals that I lived by, and that my character was equally strong. I relied on my attributes to get me through, knowing I was and am a good man, a good human being.

The Air Force Core Values are *Integrity First, Service Before Self, Excellence in All We Do.* To live these core values while in the military, I had to hide who I was. Now, I could live these core values honestly, openly. Even though I joined and served in the military being gay, I didn't look at lying about my sexuality as not living my core values. My core values don't have anything to do with who I am attracted to. I kept the Air Force Core Values intact. I lived my Air Force life with integrity and pride.

15 : What's Next?

The only way I know to be is to be open, approachable, and willing to meet new people.

I decided to move in with my family and was there for about thirty days. I wasn't sure what I wanted to do. I got a job working for Enterprise Rent-A-Car. I made some very nice friends (lights). I worked in Clayton initially then moved down the road with the company as it was growing. I remembered that the state of Illinois had grants available for military members to be able to go to college, as long as the military member was from Illinois and joined in that state. I made a few phone calls and got my Illinois State Veterans Grant started. I enrolled in Southern Illinois University at Edwardsville (SIUE).

I was excited to be going to school, especially as it was being paid for as a military benefit. I studied mass communication: television and radio broadcasting, with a minor in the German language. I was working full-time and going to school full-time. I'd put myself on the accelerated life program, as I felt I was behind my peer group. I was already thirty-one and just starting college. I went to school full-time during the summers too, which enabled me to be able to graduate in three years with a four-year degree. I maintained a decent GPA throughout.

It was during these years that I met a guy from Germany who was making his way across the country on his holiday from life. In Europe, many young people take to the wind and travel, experiencing life before they go to civil service for two years, which is required of all kids graduating high school, or to University or to get married. He was making his way across America for the first time. I met him through a girl who was in my German class that he reached out to. That chance meeting opened my life. We became best friends, and to this day, we are still friends. I've gone to Germany every year since then to travel around Europe with him. I met his family, his twin brother, and his friends, who became my friends (lights). When he did get married, I flew to Dublin to witness it. He married a girl from Ireland, and they lived in Scotland.

The friendships that were created so long ago are still with me. This was yet another testimony to my ability to make friends and sustain valued friendships throughout my life and all around the world. I've traveled to Scotland multiple times and love being with his wife and their two kids.

This was a time for me to make new connections and expand my social network. I met a guy at a gay bar I went to in St. Louis, called Magnolias. It was my first gay bar ever. I was full of anticipation because I didn't know what to expect, and to just have the feeling of people being interested in me was like a drug. I had never felt such a feeling before being around people who were like me. I went there a handful of times and met a guy who would later become my boyfriend. He and I lived together for about seven years in Edwardsville. I knew I wanted to date other guys, so we broke up and I explored my sexuality even more. I was really enjoying myself with all this newfound freedom. But I hurt him so bad, he ended up moving away. I called him one day a few years later to apologize. He was a very understanding guy. He accepted my apology and understood where I was and accepted that. We remained friends until his death.

I started dating a guy fourteen years younger than me. I loved this guy. He worked for the Botanical Gardens as a horticulturist. He was a dreamy sort that I enjoyed being around. I loved his energy and outlook on life. I used to sit in awe listening to him name both the Latin names and their English names of flowers. My emotional issues never seemed to leave me, regardless of my growth and maturity. The insecurity they brought was embarrassing and destroyed the relationships I was trying to build. He was too young and new to the gay world to deal with me and all that. He was on a different path of life. My lifestyle and his clashed. I wanted to settle more, and he didn't. The insecurities about rejection resurfaced. I thought I had pushed them down, not realizing that I'd only kept them captive. I destroyed the relationship and broke up with him.

I was finally able to name the sources of my emotional stability: rejection and looking bad were the driving factors. These were directly linked to the environment where I grew up, having never felt accepted by anyone. Rejection made me want to disappear, just as I did as a child, climbing to the top of that tree to hide. I could no longer do that. I was an adult but was emotionally inept. The fear of being rejected affected every relationship I'd had up to this point. I was also blamed for a task not being completed in the military, and it affected people at a duty weekend. I didn't take ownership of what I had done. I knew old issues were resurfacing. I thought I had handled them and put them away, but in reality, I hadn't.

My emotions were bouncing around like a pinball: wall-to-wall, top-to-bottom, all over the place. The old feelings of not being wanted or good enough came back. I thought I would try to date someone again, thinking I'd learned from mistakes I'd made in my last relationship. But I knew the feeling of not feeling worthy would stay with me unless I got guidance. Things would only change when I could be brutally honest with myself. Until then, nothing would change. I didn't have a firm foothold on my inner emotional gay being. I still felt insecure, and whenever a breakup would happen, I took it personally. I felt like I was damaged, which I was. This was the beginning of my awareness that I needed to do something or I would never have a meaningful relationship with anyone, including myself. My outward appearance and my confidence in my abilities to do a good job were conflicting with my inner self and my lack of confidence as a whole person.

I believe things happen for a reason and in the way they were meant to. I have always paid particular attention to signs from the Universe, except when it came to my personal being. I was approaching a wall full force.

The year before I graduated from college, I reentered the Air Force but in the reserves. I found out that I could do that since I was on active duty. I still wanted to get a military retirement. Scott AFB was close and that is where I was stationed. I rejoined in 1995. By this time, President Clinton had passed the Don't Ask, Don't Tell policy for the LGBTQIA+ community in the military. The law was worthless but a step closer to being changed. I was out to everyone but people in the military. It didn't really bother me much, as I wasn't dating anyone anyway. I worked at Scott AFB one weekend a month and two weeks out of the year but also had the option of doing *man-days* where I could work there every day outside the normal reservist days. I worked there to make ends meet while I finished college.

I graduated from college and had a graduation party at my apartment. A friend of mine brought her friends with her, who were lesbians. This chance meeting proved to be really powerful and awesome. She and I became friends. We stayed in touch and communicated a lot about everything. We got to know each other very well. She became my confidant and my English expert. She has a gift for grammar, structure, and words and how it all worked together. I loved talking with her and discovering new words, just listening

Steve and his best friend Mary, 2017.

to her. She corrects me if I use a word or phrase incorrectly. I love that. She and her girlfriend broke up about a year later, but she and I really bonded as I helped her through that. Our friendship was solid.

After I graduated, I landed a full-time job with UPS as an account executive. This was the first time I made real money. I mean, my paycheck was equivalent to three months of my military salary. I was never motivated by money, but it was nice to have those paychecks. This was a short-lived experience, as I was looking around for a job that I didn't have to live in other places, commute to Scott AFB, and maintain my lifestyle in St. Louis. Working in Columbia, Missouri, with UPS didn't work out.

Being in the reserves, I made my next rank as the slot I filled required me to hold that rank. I steadily increased my knowledge, went to a few military leadership courses in Biloxi, Mississippi, and took on a few assignments and job upgrade training sessions until I had all I needed to move up to each new rank. I would fulfill my one weekend a month and two weeks out of the year and embraced my role with the military. I loved wearing my uniform again. I could see the bigger picture of retiring. I wanted this achievement, so I stayed the course. I loved the Air Force and what I gained from it. I was on my own, single and ready to bring new adventures into my life.

I got my own place and was living alone. I went to a bar called The Loading Zone with my friend Danny. It became a regular thing for the two of us to hang out on Tuesday nights and enjoy show tunes, as Tuesday nights were known as *Show Tune Tuesdays*. We had a great time. We would meet there every Tuesday night to have drinks. One night, out of the blue, this guy introduced himself to me and we started talking. He told me he thought I was unlike anyone he had ever met. I was flattered. He and I hit it off instantly.

The euphoric stage is always the best part—that stage where no one really knows the other. We were enthralled by our newness, which drove the euphoria. I knew I still had emotional issues but also needed the validation of someone else liking me. That desire overwhelmed my need to comprehend my emotional state of mind. I dove into the relationship, moving into his house with him, and we ended up wanting to get a house together. We searched the St. Louis City area and ended up in a neighborhood called the

Gate District. We stopped in to see the display home, talked with the sales staff, and both fell in love with the Compton model.

At that time, Mayor Slay had a project in the city to revitalize this blighted neighborhood. That made us feel more comfortable about making an appointment with the salespeople to solidify getting our dream home started. This decision proved to be a major step forward for me. I had never built a home before, let alone one of this size. We built the house, the first time for the both of us to have a contractor build a home that we designed. The house had a little over 3,600 square feet of livable space. We also finished the basement. While the house was being built, we decided to add an in-ground pool on the side of the house and had a six-foot privacy fence put up, surrounding the sides and back of the house and flanking off the front. We decided to do that so the neighborhood kids and the public couldn't see the pool and prevent people from getting in it for safety and liability reasons.

At that time, the president of the St. Vincent Park neighborhood association got her board together and sent us a letter telling us we couldn't put up a solid white fence around our yard and that we had to take down what had already been put up because it didn't fit with the historical aspect of the neighborhood. The fence had to be a black wrought iron fence that could be seen through. We couldn't have that as we had an attractive nuisance, a pool. The neighborhood covenants and bylaws didn't cover anything like a pool. My partner and I had a meeting with the St. Louis Development Corporation (SLDC) in response to the letter from the neighborhood president, and we successfully argued to keep the fence. I was told that I did an excellent job of presenting and defending the issues.

This prompted the SLDC representative to ask me to think about running for president of my neighborhood association when it opened up again. I had never thought about anything like that, and my partner said I should consider this, based on how well I handled the meeting and presented arguments. When the president's position opened up, I ran. To my surprise, I won. It was an affirming acknowledgment of my tact, professionalism, confidence, and compassion to do the right thing.

I ended up negotiating with the Board of Alderman to get the infrastructure of our neighborhood set up and running, including getting the alleys paved, dumpsters placed with a schedule of pickups, and streets and curbing put in with defined easements from the streets to the yards; the sidewalks were redone; street cleaning crews were set up to routinely make the neighborhood part of its weekly pickup; and the police made routine passes. I also organized to have the city plant trees. Within a year, this newly built neighborhood was functioning as never before. Monthly meetings kept the neighbors updated on our progress as well as the houses still being built. One house was an eyesore, so I had it taken down. The neighbors gave me a brick from that house as a thank you gift for having it removed.

Next, I created a neighborhood watch program, which got the attention of the president of the Board of Alderman. Every ten houses had a block captain, and by going house to house, I got phone numbers and email addresses to create a phone tree to keep the neighborhood safe and help communicate if anyone saw anything suspicious. The emails I used to send correspondence and updates throughout the month also let them know when the next meetings would be.

I was proud of all the work and coordination. The crime stats that once hovered high over this neighborhood dropped down to five percent due to organizing and getting the residents of the neighborhood involved. We all had a vested interest living here. The monthly meetings, rather than being a waste of time, provided opportunities for people to share ideas, and I also shared what the association and I were doing each month to keep everyone on the same page.

After a few years, my partner and I broke up. I realized at this point that the baggage people bring to a relationship is more powerful to destroy than keep it together. I was making decent money to maintain my lifestyle, so I bought out his portion of the house. It was a bit more than I needed, but nevertheless, I bought him out and lived there for another eight years, proving to myself once again that I could do it on my own. Even though this was a challenge, I knew I was up for it.

This success and validation should have added to my mental strength, the strength I used to push back all the insecurities and hatred inflicted on me growing up. But it wasn't. It occurred to me it might be time to stop pushing back and time to start letting go of all that.

16 : A Whole New Basic Training

I have always vibrated at a higher frequency than most!

Getting involved in neighborhood policies and projects proved to be a natural fit for me. After my time as St. Vincent Park president, the president position of the Gate District became available. I was asked by the entire neighborhood if I would run for that position. I did and won that one too. I was now the president of an entire district. My leadership qualities were never in question. My personality, mixed with what I learned in the military, became a win for me and all the residents in this district. Over seven hundred households made up these four neighborhoods: St. Vincent Park, Eads Park, Buder Park, and Lafayette Terrace. It was wonderful overseeing the growth of the district as a whole. My board and I made decisions on new businesses and new housing going up, always keeping in mind property values and the integrity of the historical aspect of the district.

I was growing mentally, and as I became more aware of people, I could see them even more clearly. I understood the different choices people made and how they live out those choices. My Aunt Agnes died in 1989, and the priest gave her eulogy. I remember him saying how terrible it was that she never married and had no children to carry on. Even though Aunt Agnes was the one who first called me sissy, to hear the priest say that made me angry, and I thought he was an ass for saying that. Not everyone chooses that path.

Fast-forward to when another aunt passed, Aunt Rose. I decided I wanted to tell about her life from my perspective, as someone who loved and knew her. I wrote her eulogy and delivered it at her funeral mass in church. I felt that someone who knew her should talk on her behalf instead of a scripted speech with no feeling or meaning in it, like that with my Aunt Agnes. I was never one to hold a grudge but always looked for the good—sometimes to a fault. I gave her a beautiful eulogy despite how I'd been treated. People told me that I captured Aunt Rose's essence perfectly. From then on, I wrote all the eulogies on my dad's side of the family, trying to do the same thing for each of them. It got to the point where each person wanted to hear what I thought of them and how I saw them before they passed because they said they wouldn't be able to hear it. So, the idea came to me to send them their story for their birthday. For one full year, as each birthday rolled around, I wrote their story containing their essence, bought a birthday card, put the story in it, and mailed it. People loved how I saw and described them and how they touched my life. This was another time where being selfless in giving and using my people and writing skills was appreciated. Everyone in my family, including a few aunts on my mom's side, and very close friends of mine all appreciated receiving their story except for a few. They thought I wrote nothing but lies. I laughed because I write about the beautiful things I see in people. I guess they couldn't see what I saw in them. Even so, given the pain they inflicted on me, I was glad I could still see the goodness in them.

It was time to work on myself. I wasn't sure how that would appear for me, but I knew I had to work on my emotional well-being. I knew the Universe would provide grace and be diligent, always watching over me. Sure enough, someone was placed in my life who would change my course. A friend introduced me to this very nice guy from Pittsburgh at Mardi Gras in St. Louis. Mardi Gras is a big deal in S. Louis; it holds the second largest celebration outside of New Orleans. We hung out all day and really got to know each other. After a few times together, we started dating. He had such a gentle spirit about him. Even my mom commented about that. I recognized his laid-back nature and insight into others as attributes I needed in my life. Eventually, he moved into my home, and we shared everything.

Although I was sort of out in the military, I didn't talk about it. With this man, I was finally comfortable with my sexuality. He was a gift from the Universe. He could see I was struggling with some deep emotional issues, my inner conflicts. He saw them and knew I was fighting myself. He had gone through some personal development courses about a year before meeting me, which he said had helped him deal with his own baggage. At first, I pushed back, but then remembered I was seeking something just like this.

He asked, "How long have you been trying to fix yourself?"

I replied, "For quite a long time now."

That made me think. I had accomplished a great deal up to this point, developing my leadership strengths and resolve. I thought about the advice I had given to people throughout my military career and my civilian life. I was always looking for ways to support others and improve situations, offering different ways of thinking about things. I was delivering good advice but wasn't living it. With my partner's encouragement, I enrolled in an experiential learning program, initially created by Werner Erhard. In 2006, I began to repair the damaged areas in myself. I started my journey in the personal development class. This course is no longer available, but did it ever make a difference in my life. I started in the Basic course designed to bring me closer to myself. Facing myself, with myself, I uncovered the parts of my damaged psyche. Putting them on the table to be dissected, I learned how I felt about myself.

The second course was called Advanced. This course was designed to take what was uncovered in the basic course and advance it to a better understanding of myself. It gave me the confidence I needed to overcome the insecurities I'd been harboring all my life. Each of the participants was given a song by our instructors. I was given the song *Proud* by Heather Small to define my inner being.

Ownership Program (OP) was the last phase of this workshop. The first two courses were an intense eight-hours-a-day, weeklong exercise. OP is three months long. Every day I worked on myself, journaled, and talked each morning with a mentor assigned to me. Talking with my mentor was a powerful way to start my days. Throughout this three-month period, I went through many intensive exercises to stay on track with and develop myself. I recognized the feelings of diminished self-worth and rejection I felt each time someone moved on and understood why they were in my psyche. The self-torment of not feeling worthy was laid on a table. I felt the rage I'd been covering up and released the hurt and anger by pushing them away from me instead of blaming myself. I sent the projections from others back to them.

This new awareness didn't happen overnight, but once I took the time to understand the barriers I had created to protect myself, I could let them go. I was a work in progress for a while, but with the help of the counselors and fellow participants in my class, I released the pain and understood its origin. The support and encouragement I received was nothing short of a miracle.

At the end of the course, we traveled to an undisclosed location for our retreat weekend. We were assigned a room with a roommate who was in the course with us. There were, I think, eight of us in this course. We were all at the peak of our learning. The exercises we were going through consisted of digging deeply within ourselves to flush out anything that might not have been uncovered in the previous training.

Our final assignment was to take a walk through the woods, find something that spoke to us, and write about how we identified with it as specifically as we could. The project was designed for each of us to do this alone. I was walking, looking for something that spoke to me. Nearing the end of my walk, I looked to my left and there it was. Like a warm light, I was drawn to this boulder that was sitting there, with a tree growing out of a crack that was in the rock. I had found my lesson. The following is what I wrote:

> You are the most beautiful thing. I saw you alone and rooted firmly in a boulder, persevering and trying your hardest to stay alive. You didn't need help from anything or any other tree. You are your own strength and nourishment. You are a tree, hoping someday to provide protection for anyone seeking shelter from the world. Although you are small right now, you have the potential to be huge, and as you grow, break apart the boulder so you can thrive but not threaten. Your beauty will be enough to WOW onlookers. You are not flamboyant or have flowers, but you're still the most

beautiful thing to me. I saw you and you saw me; you and I both know what you represent, and I was coming for you to gaze upon your strength. You and I are very much alike, not just surviving but thriving against all odds. Your tiny leaves are swaying from the breeze that happens to come by once in a while. You don't ask for much, just a beam of sunshine, a little rain, and a nice breeze. The rest you do on your own. You are a strong little tree, and someday you will be tall and beautiful. Don't be frightened or intimidated by the bigger trees around you. You are unique and have a beautiful force all your own, that's what makes you unique, and you. I love you, little tree, you are surviving for the sake of surviving and what you mean to me. We are both surviving, on our own and not hurting anyone in the process.

We turned our stories of the lesson each of us found into the instructors. We were all called back into the room, and one story was chosen that stood out from the rest. It was my story of the little tree. They read it aloud and said that of all the stories they had received in their courses, my story struck a chord because it was so personal and true to my life. We graduated from this course, and we went back to our lives living a cleaner, healthier life, having released the insecurities we had arrived with. These insecurities will always try to show themselves, but the tools each participant received will help and guide us through the times when we feel vulnerable. I finished this course in June 2007.

Years later, when I decided to write this book, I wanted to find a boulder with a tree growing out

This tree found strength to survive all odds, as Steve did.

of it so I could put a photo of it in my book. I found my boulder in Forest Park where I run or walk in the mornings.

My partner and I were nearing the end of our relationship. He was hired to work in a new position in Manhattan with his company. We commuted for about six months, then on my final visit to see him one weekend, we had a talk and decided it was time to end the relationship. It was the best, most healthy breakup I had ever experienced. It was almost like a handshake, but it wasn't. We hugged and parted. I asked him if he would deliver the invocation at my retirement from the Air Force Reserve. He said he would.

If it weren't for the courses I had taken, I would have destroyed that relationship too. Instead, we are still friends today. The norm in my life had been to take breakups personally, as if I weren't good enough, but I'd learned that it is OK for people to move on, that everyone is on their specific journey in life, including me. It was not a reflection of me or what makes me beautiful inside. I was strong enough to hold myself accountable if I wronged someone, especially in the relationship. Instead of making it about myself, I realized everyone is on their own journey through this life, and we learn as we go along. People will always come and go; lessons are always learned and left behind in any situation. By finding my strengths and affirming "Steve really is a good guy," I was able to evaluate my thoughts and decisions and finally learn to trust myself.

The lessons I learned being with my partner, especially from his laid-back demeanor, will be with me for a lifetime. I will be forever grateful for his love, friendship, and the gift of who he is. By introducing the opportunity to change my behavior through these courses, he gave me the gift of myself. He loved me enough and could see what kind of a man I was.

He told me, "You are a great guy. Let's get your mental well-being fixed. People need to experience the goodness of your love." He told me this before I started these courses.

Outside the military and other things I accomplished, being with him and participating in three life-changing courses ranked right up there with joining the military as one of the most fulfilling decisions I'd ever made for myself. They helped me be a better person. I still go through challenging times, sometimes losing my way, but I have a solid foundation I can rely on to get me back on track quickly. Struggles and discontent will always present themselves, but now I get through them with a healthier mindset.

17 : Another Retirement

Get on the field of life and play; stay off the sidelines, watching. If you fall, get up and try again; if you succeed, help the others who haven't quite made it that far. In any event, play, laugh, sing, travel, fall, get hurt, love again, and most importantly, love who you are becoming and who you are and embrace everything about yourself with acceptance.

I had served enough years in the Air Force Reserve to be able to retire, with my culminating experience as Career Advisor for the Maintenance group at Scott AFB. In November of 2007, I retired as a Master Sergeant (E7). At one point in my career, I had thought this was unattainable. I was now part of the top three echelon of the enlisted force. It was a big deal. I retired with a chest full of medals and commendations, my track of ribbons and medals containing fifteen such awards. I earned everything on my uniform chest, from rank to awards and medals. I'm very proud of what I did in the Air Force. I miss wearing my uniform because of what I earned while in the Air Force, both active duty and reserve. Like my bachelor's degree, no one can take these achievements away from me. I am proud of my service and everything it has given me. I served in this position for three years. Of all the positions I held in the Air Force, this one was the most growth inspiring, both for my personal development and the development of the troops I served. I had an open-door policy, so all could come to me and talk about their career paths or personal issues. I became a friend they could come to whom they could trust. I learned a great deal in this position for my own mental well-being. This is the best job I had ever held in the Air Force because it offered me the opportunity to interact on a personal level with all the service members. The airmen and sergeants and a few officers I worked with followed my advice and advanced in their careers and in their personal lives. I have letters from many of these folks thanking me, letting me know the influence I had in their lives, and that they will never forget how I helped them. They identified my kindness, understanding, empathy, and care. Most importantly, they trusted me to guide them in a direction I would be willing to travel myself. Like them, I was coming into my own every day, having grown so much in the positions I'd held as a civilian and throughout my military career. The growth from my personal achievements outside the military were also in play here. Learning ways to identify and work with the demons that held me back or kept me from feeling balanced became growth strategies I shared to help others address their own inner struggles.

Steve's retirement from the Air Force, 2007.

Steve's medals and ribbons from serving his country proudly in the
United States Air Force.

That final summer I was president of the District, I invited the mayor of the
city to attend our National Night Out. He came, and we talked for a while
about the progress the neighborhood was experiencing by including new
businesses moving in. He thanked me for all the hard work my board and
I did to get the new neighborhood up to par and to maintain the other three
neighborhoods that were already established. He said if I needed anything
to call his office. This was the first time we had met. I was blessed to have
such wonderful people on my boards. I couldn't have been as successful
as a leader without their support behind me. The mayor told me he was
sad to see me step down but knew I had done a lot and that he was very
glad I had been in these positions when it was so crucial. I was proud of all
I had accomplished.

On November 2, 2007, a week prior to my retirement date, the President
of the Board of Alderman presented me with a Resolution from the City
of St. Louis recognizing all I had accomplished in the neighborhoods,
leading the boards I had headed up to successfully build and then maintain
the District in high standing with the city, and acknowledging my pending
retirement from the Air Force. Now, on November 2 each year, I have my
name for that day in the city forever. I am very proud of that. Many lights
were added to my meadow from these ex

My intention is to stay true to my values of doing the right thing—not just
for myself, but for others. When I work for others, helping out, it gives me
satisfaction, a deep fulfillment, far more than anything else I do. I believe we
are put here on earth to help and serve others in any capacity we can. There

is no better way to feel good or proud of yourself than to give of yourself to others. I knew this about me as a kid, and I stayed true to myself, holding onto this aspect of my being, even when others behaved differently.

Even though so many good things were happening on the civilian side of my life, I was feeling sad about leaving the military, this institution that had given me so much in return for all I had given to it. I love my country, and being in the military transformed my life. Now I was beginning another phase and was even better prepared because of my military experience. I knew in my heart it was time to end this chapter in my life and move to the next level.

Throughout my military career, I supervised a number of individuals. I guided them in their careers and made sure I gave them whatever I could to help them succeed. While holding positions of leadership, I discovered that this was an innate quality in me. Growing up, my parents and most of my family didn't think I had it in me to be strong. The conflict of being the eldest while being made to feel like I was the youngest had a detrimental impact on my psyche. I struggled many years with this duality, fighting the personal insecurities that grew out of my childhood. It was only as an adult that I was able to overcome them and be what the Universe intended all along: a leader.

There is a gift in being able to be seen and respected for who you are and what you bring to the table. Many people I have met through the years, outside my family, see me for who I am, and the respect they give and show me is not overlooked or taken for granted. But some behaviors of people who have not grown in their own awareness reflect this lack, and I see them, so I keep my distance. I stand firm on truth and justice. If those are not respected or demonstrated by others, I stand up for it and make it right. In the roles I held as leader, I was fair, kind, and understanding and never once did I abuse that role, as others counted on me and looked up to me to give good advice and guidance. This is another aspect of my personality that I gained from the military. *Keeping my word is paramount.* Fairness is in my DNA and also part of my libra sign. I now let people know, "If it isn't fair, I'll make it fair, and someone isn't going to like it."

By the time my tour of duty as president was winding down, I knew I didn't want to run for another term. I turned over my authority. I took a break from community service to focus on my job. I worked in logistics shipping blood and medical products around the nation and abroad with a same-day, door-to-door shipping service. I worked from home. Service for people is where I am the strongest. This job was no different.

To add to my already strong sense of accomplishment, a neighbor gave me a letter, summing me up in this statement:

> "To say you understand people and care for others charitably would be an understatement. You are the kind of gem that people spend years trying to find. A deeply compassionate soul, you love and help others altruistically. You have a genuine affection that is easily recognizable and highly commendable. Honestly, we'd all want nothing more than to have more of you in this world."

Throughout my life, I have had gifts like this given to me by people who understand the world and recognize the beauty in not just me, but people in general. From early on, my nieces and nephews have given me beautiful gifts like this because they trusted me and loved me unconditionally. I have everything they have ever given to me: notes, pictures they drew, letters, etc. I keep all of it close to my heart. They felt comfortable and trusted me more than they did their parents much of the time. I unconditionally offered them a space where they were free to be themselves and could talk with me about anything.

Mary and I have been friends for over twenty-six years now. Outside of a few family members, she knows me the best on this earth. She and I can talk about everything, anytime. My cousin Dana and I have always been close too. These two women, along with Little Mary, were my support group. They helped me through some pretty rough times in my life. I protect that connection and trust it, holding it in my heart. A bit later they would perform a vital role in my life to get me through the toughest challenge I would ever face. They are angels on earth for me. I just hope I was able to serve in this capacity for them at some point in their life. Going through the personal development courses helped me identify and reduce a lot of the insecurities I'd shared with them. I value and will always protect the relationships I have with each of them.

18 : Life on My Terms

"Put into the world the beauty of being yourself and the healthy energy you bring."
~ Steve Zeiger

I was newly single and enjoying my alone time. Retired from the military and no longer leading the district, I was free to relax for a while, so I focused on my sales and marketing job in logistics.

I was an executive sales representative selling same-day, door-to-door services to the blood banking industry, which led to medical devices, clinical trials, transporting of organs. The company I worked for contracted through commercial airlines to accomplish the door-to-door service. I shipped products both domestically and internationally and made massive progress financially from it. I loved the fact I was helping people survive with the products I was charged with shipping.

I was living life on my terms but still dealing with acceptance in my own family. By 2012, I wanted to get more involved in the LGBTQIA+ community. Being a military retiree and gay, I felt I had a great deal to offer as a role model and mentor to help others feel proud to live in this country, especially those who were gay and serving or who wanted to serve and be free to be themselves. I started volunteering at the LGBTQIA+ Community Center. Pride was coming, and I thought it was time to bring the military to Pride.

I organized a group of people to carry the branch flags in the parade. I reached out to the organizers of the Pride event through a friend who worked there. He got me in touch with the organizers; they said, "yes, by all means, bring it." I went to Scott AFB and bought all the branch flags and the American flag. I then went to Home Depot to see if I could find flag poles. They didn't have any so I bought paint poles, extended them out, and taped them with packing tape so they wouldn't collapse on themselves. I drilled holes in the poles to run a zip tie through to attach the flags. The next thing I did was create a T-shirt with the name of each branch on it. With my elements set, I searched for veterans and found five volunteers to carry the flags. When Pride came around, we walked in that parade with the flags flying. This was the first time this had been done in the nation, as far as I knew. The crowd went ecstatic when they saw us carrying them. I was so proud of this I could hardly contain my tears. It was a wonderful moment. I knew I had even more to give to not just the LGBTQIA+ community but to the whole population.

When Pride was over, Ellen, a new friend (light) of mine and the parade director for Pride St. Louis, said how proud she was to see this element in the parade. Her father was retired Air Force too, and it made her weep seeing us. I asked her if I could get more involved. She said yes, and that they had their annual election board meeting in August each year. She said I should come to the next meeting and interview.

They invited me, but a few days prior to that Monday meeting, I had a bike accident and broke my wrist. I went to the meeting in a lot of pain with my lower arm in a cast, so I didn't sell myself well and I wasn't elected to be on the board. Ellen encouraged me to come back the next year and try

Steve holds the Air Force flag at PrideFest, 2012.

again. So, I did, and I had a great idea to propose. That next year, Pride was being moved to downtown St. Louis to be held on the street where the Soldiers Memorial sits. I thought about this location, my military background, my identity as LGBTQIA+, and all the men and women who served in past conflicts, sometimes giving their lives for this country, never being able to be completely free about who they were because of bigotry and some religious doctrine dictating who they had to be rather than who they were. The more I thought about this, the more the idea came to me to hold a wreath-laying ceremony at the Soldiers Memorial honoring all those who served in silence about who they were and how they were not allowed to be proud of who they really were because of the times in which they lived. I decided we needed to honor them with a wreath created in rainbow colors with each branch represented on the wreath.

The first Pride wreath in front of the cenotaph at Soldiers Memorial.

I made a few phone calls to find out who I needed to speak with at the Soldiers Memorial. I was given the name of the superintendent, Lynnea. She and I talked about what I wanted to create at the Memorial for Pride. She was in complete support of my idea and made the entire museum available for me to utilize. The electric, microphones, extra flags—she did everything she could do to help me create this beautiful ceremony. She was thrilled when I let her know I wanted to light the top of the Memorial in Pride colors. Her help was valued deeply as this was the first time it had ever been done in the City of St. Louis. She even made the comment, "This will be a first in the nation!"

I presented the idea to the Pride Board as a brand-new entry. They loved it so much that, instead of having it placed somewhere else during Pride, they decided to open the 2013 Pride with this event. I was allowed to put on this entire ceremony. I had the wreath created by the florist Walter Knoll who gave me a deal, as I didn't have any money for it. I wanted to light the Soldiers Memorial in rainbow colors but had no money for that either. As this was a new event, it wasn't in the Pride budget, so I had to get money. I asked friends and some family to donate toward the lighting. Then I went online and found Nick at Ironman Sound Industries.

After I explained to Nick what I wanted to have done, I told him, "I would like to have you do the lights. What bid can you give me?"

 "How much of the Memorial do you want to light up?" Nick asked.

"Just the top of it, since I didn't have a budget this year. And we'll commit to using your company next year, if you can give me a deal this first time."

He said, "Sure! I'll charge you $500 for this year."

I had my rainbow lights if I could raise the money. I held a fundraiser at Honey, a new gay bar in the Grove, which was the gay strip in St. Louis. The theme I created was a USO party with drag queens as the Andrews Sisters and cigarette girls. The bar was decked out as a 1940's canteen. One of the other bars let me use their camouflage netting. With support from the gay community, I was able to raise a little over $500 dollars, which was enough to pay Ironman Sound.

USO Party flyer.

I had it all set with all the players except for people to carry the flags. I called each recruiting office to see if they would be able to send one person over to carry their flag. They did. This was the era of President Obama, and LGBTQIA+ marriage and equality rights had been passed. One by one, the states were passing legal marriages, and it seemed like we could finally be free to love and be as we were, with complete acceptance. It wasn't difficult to find people to participate from the military.

I was able to find a bugler to play Taps, write a speech, and enlist the first speaker, whom I knew and was a colonel in the Army Air Corps in WWII, which in 1947 became the Air Force. I found a DJ to play the national anthem and songs appropriate for the ceremony. The day came for this to happen. All players were in place: the flag bearers, the bugler to play Taps, music playing the national anthem, and the wreath.

I delivered a moving speech to all who were witnessing history. I was so proud of all that had been done; every moment was emblazoned in my memory. I knew this would be the true beginning of all things possible in this country for people who live their lives being marginalized. I recognized this opportunity to help people feel proud of themselves and do great things, like serve their country. I thought it was time to show the world that we are all here to make a difference and have beautiful things to contribute to the world. I am grateful I had the strength, wisdom, and creativity to do my part to recognize the LGBTQIA+ members of our society and grateful beyond words for the City of St. Louis, the

Soldiers Memorial lit in Pride colors. Photo by Scott Lokitz.

Soldiers Memorial, and Pride St. Louis to allow me to bring this dream to reality for the nation, all starting in St. Louis.

In my speech, and all subsequent speeches, I talk about the honor of serving our country. But I've added the following: "We serve our country with pride and distinction. We don't go in the military protecting just one social or class segment of the country, like the white male, Black female, or one specific religious group. We serve everyone collectively, protecting the rights of all citizens, so they are treated fairly and equally." The wreath-laying ceremony opened Pride in 2013, with the following as my speech:

Steve in full uniform at the podium ready to deliver his speech.

WITNESSING HISTORY

Today you are recognized, therefore you are free! Freedom.

History is being made today! Take a look around at where you are for Pride this year. Yes, at a wreath-laying ceremony at the Soldiers Memorial to honor the LGBTQIA+ service members who fought and paid the ultimate price for this great country. We are making history today, folks.

This is the first time ever that this is happening, and it's about time, I might add! Throughout the history of this great country, different segments of the population had to fight and rally and protest to be treated fairly and recognized by the government. Whether it was child labor, a woman's right to vote, Black people being treated fairly and equal, or now the gays and lesbians being recognized and being treated fairly, to have the right to marry and be equal to their heterosexual counterparts, with all the benefits that come along with being married. With DOMA and Prop 8 falling, we are now equal in the eyes of the law. Yay!!

As a retired master sergeant from the Air Force and a gay man, I can tell you the feeling I have is breathtaking. To be able to stand before you, dedicate a wreath to the fallen LGBTQIA+ members, and to speak openly about who I am is nothing short of remarkable. This ceremony today is not just for the military alive and dead, but for all my brothers and sisters who make up the LGBTQIA+ community. You have the right, now, to truly be all you want to be, in the military, if you choose to.

I am honored to have a retired Air Force colonel in the ceremony today to help dedicate this wreath with me. He is a World War II veteran who served for thirty-nine years. In his years, he has seen many changes; this change to the LGBTQIA+ community has special meaning for him. His grandson, Colin Lovett, is the president of the LGBTQIA+

Center of St. Louis. I couldn't think of a better person to dedicate this wreath to the fallen with me than a fellow brother in arms.

Today, we honor all the men and women who identified as LGBTQIA+ and served this country; some also died doing so, quietly, afraid to tell their brothers and sisters in arms who they were, and not truly having that feeling of being an equal warrior because of their sexuality, even though they fought and died next to one another. I find it odd for anyone to think we can give our lives for this country and not be considered equal. We fought and fight for the rights for everyone to be free, not just certain segments of the population. We are Americans; we are ALL free. If that doesn't resonate in you, I have a copy of the constitution I'd be happy to share with you so you can read up on it.

To all the veterans, including the LGBTQIA+ members who paid the ultimate price, and whose names are etched on these walls in tribute, we salute you. I am your voice today. Thank you for your service and defending the rights of Americans to be free and for all peoples around the world who you fought for so they could win their independence too. Today, you're recognized, therefore you are free!

Thank you for your service. This is for you, and for every citizen of this great nation!

We then placed the wreath, Taps was played, and both the colonel and I rendered salutes to the wreath in front of the cenotaph.

The significance of bringing together the Soldiers Memorial mission and PrideFest is that we claimed/established a place for LGBTQIA+ vets within the mission, a purpose that will never be undone.

The mission statement for the Soldiers Memorial Military Museum is:

Focusing on the St. Louis area both past and present...
To honor the service and sacrifice of our military, our veterans,

and their families; To document and to facilitate learning about the military experience, the veteran experience, and the wartime experience on the battlefront and on the St. Louis home front.

That wreath ceremony made us equal in the eyes of everyone who has served and who is serving. After all, we served together with one mission and passion in mind, preserving our freedoms, not just in America, but freeing people from dictators who don't respect human rights around the world. If we are equal on the battlefield, we will be equal at home as well.

This was an important moment in time, and I had the privilege to present it with great pride and honor. I was passionate about creating a memory for all to remember. The Pride Board loved what I had created. When I went back to apply for a position on the board, they unanimously agreed to vote me on. I became the Operations Director with a Military Element attached for two years, which turned into three years. Each year, I invited a new guest speaker, the flag bearers, a bugler for Taps, and the DJ as part of the ceremony. The wreath was created each year and the entire Soldiers Memorial was lit in full Pride colors.

By the third year, I got the attention of Boeing and their LGBTQIA+ component. Their LGBTQIA+ representative approached me and said they would like to sponsor this element at Pride. I was thrilled to have them pick up the costs for lighting and the wreath. And finally, I was able to replace my paint poles with real flag poles.

The John J. Cochran Veterans Hospital, of the VA in St. Louis, wanted to be involved too, so they put up a booth at Pride and also walked in the parade. These were all firsts for the city and the nation. I was invited to go to the VA and speak about being gay and how vital our roles are in the military. I thought this would be an appropriate time to reach out to Scott AFB in Illinois and inquire about being part of their Diversity Day Celebration too. After contacting their Diversity Board, they agreed it would be a great idea, especially since President Obama had lifted all discriminatory bans and LGBTQIA+ people were allowed to be married legally. Policies and regulations were also changing in the military, so I started attending their meetings. By the time their Diversity Day rolled around at the end of the month, I was able to put up my Pride tent with flags and educational items for people to take. The Pride tent sat between the Hispanic Heritage and Women's Month tent. We had many visitors to the tent. The overall response to us being there was well received. We felt, and so did the board, that it was a welcomed presence. I was allowed to get on stage and speak about what this inclusion meant to the armed forces and to society and am now invited back each year. It was thrilling for me to see our tent up with the rainbow flags flying proudly on the base from which I'd retired.

The Veterans Hospital staff approached me to help start their LGBTQIA+ awareness program in St. Louis. I was invited to sit on that board and speak at their forums to bring awareness and equal treatment to all LGBTQIA+ service members and employees. At one point I was either leading or participating in four boards. I proudly gave my best to all of them.

In 2014, I approached Lynnea at the Soldiers Memorial with another request. I wanted to walk in the Veterans Day Parade with our PrideFest element. She said, "It is time for this element to be represented in the Veterans Day Parade." I presented the idea to the chairman and the board of the Veterans Day Parade. They overwhelmingly agreed to have me and this element walk in the parade. The city was in full agreement as well.

Steve driving a golf cart at PrideFest.

Between these three entities, we would walk openly in the Veterans Day Parade. For this walk, I added the rainbow flags on either end to represent and let the public know who and what we represented. The city Events Planning office contacted me to let me know my position in the parade. When the day came, we were all full of anticipation and nerves. I made sure to be there with the flags and the participants to carry each of the flags. I remember starting to walk and how proud I was to be walking in this parade and the reason for being there. I wasn't sure how people would receive us. The folks walking with me looked at me for strength, so I never let on that I was nervous about it. We walked with our heads held high. Everything was going fine as we walked, and then we paraded by the reviewing stand. Our element was called out: the LGBTQIA+ military element of St Louis. I can still hear them saying that. I was so proud, the nervousness started to disappear. We were still walking, and in the distance, I could see what looked like hundreds of bikers and everyone who hung out with them. I immediately got nervous again, and little did I know, so did the other walkers. Walking with pride and our heads high, I marched carrying the American flag with the branches walking behind me. We approached the bikers, and out of the corner of my eye, I saw this lady in her black leather stand up and start clapping. That carried through the entire ranks of the bikers. They stood up, yelled, and clapped for us. The tears were starting to well up, but I kept it together, my head held high. The pride and acceptance I felt took my breath away. The others with me held their heads high as we marched. I have never felt so accomplished on this level in my life, especially from these folks. It still brings tears to my eyes as I write this, remembering that moment. When it was over, we gathered at the end of the parade route with a huge sense of accomplishment, knowing what we had just done and the response that was generously given. We all talked about that feeling and what we had just experienced, which was another first for the nation.

As we were standing there talking, a few of these folks came up to me and said, "Congratulations and thank you for representing EVERYONE who is in the military. Most people think it's just straight people. It's not. The ranks of the military are made up of every type of citizen this country has to offer, which is why we are the greatest nation." They, too, had and have members in the armed forces who identify as LGBTQIA+. They shook my hand. I stood there just taking in that moment, moved beyond belief.

In 2014, I also created a military/Pride dog tag. I sent my idea to the patents office in Washington D.C., where they copyrighted my dog tag so that I could have them reproduced and sold.

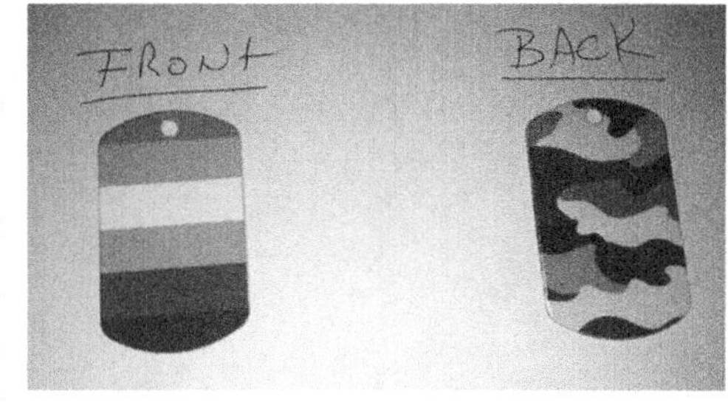

Dog tags, 2014.

I have always known that I vibrate at a higher frequency than most. This is the time that that statement is much more than words. All I'd done, striving to improve myself, now placed me on the public stage where I could influence public opinion with actions and conviction, letting everyone who participates in or just observes the ceremonies know that they, too, should be proud of who they are, regardless of what others think. The older I get, the more I accept my calling and realize the capacity I have to make things happen, in a positive way, where memories are made and remembered.

The mayor of St. Louis, the city directors, and public figures who sat on different boards had taken notice of me. When the mayor saw me, he said, "I think I know you." I replied, "Yes, sir, you do. I was the president of one of your districts in the city, the Gate District." He said, "Yes, that's right." He and I had already established a small familiarity with each other due to that role. He thanked me for bringing this element not just to the city, but also to the region, and for the difference I was making on the perception of the population toward the LGBTQIA+ community.

19 : The Gift of Awareness

I have read this story over and over. I know my life matters, not just to me, but to the world that needs kind, gentle, generous people like me. I am viable and worthy.

Once the parade was complete and the books were closed for another year, the Veterans Day Parade Committee told me they enjoyed watching me during the wreath-laying ceremony at Pride and walking in the parade. They admired my energy and said they needed younger blood who could move the board and the Soldiers Memorial into the twenty-first century with modern ideas like the military Pride element.

The chairman of the board asked if I would like to be a sitting member of the Veterans Day Committee. I answered, "I would like that." I served for a year. After that year was complete, the chairman position opened up. The sitting chairman of the board and another board member asked, "Would you consider running for the position as chairman of the board?"

"Yes," I said, "I would." So, I did and was elected chairman of the board for the Veterans Day Parade for the City of St. Louis. I was so honored. It was another first-time achievement for a gay military man to hold such a position for the City of St. Louis and in the nation. I served as chairman of the board for four years.

The third year I served was the city's 250th anniversary of becoming a city in the state. I thought we needed to include the Native American tribes who were settled here before the French settled it. I contacted all the tribes who originated here and invited them to be part of the parade, which most of them did. This was personally very satisfying and mutually rewarding. They walked in the parade with the American Veterans, holding their banners. When I create ideas and events, I bring the perspective that we all matter as citizens in this great nation, and we must honor its first inhabitants, the Indigenous peoples.

To top off a successful four years, and my final year as chairman, I was awarded the distinct honor of being Grand Marshall of the parade. I thought back over all the things I'd accomplished, given the different levels of confidence I'd had and my developing self-awareness, and realized I'd never felt like this before. I'd created a memorable life for myself, not to mention the memories created for everyone else.

During this time, St. Louis was bidding to see if the OutGames would come to our city. There were two other cities bidding. This gave me an interesting idea. In the middle of all the things I was working on and the boards I sat on, I'd also honed my line dancing skills and created a line dance group, the St. Louis

Steve receiving a plaque as Grand Marshall of the Veterans Day Parade, 2016.

Stompers. I thought it would be cool to participate in these games. With the help of the DJ, we put our team together and started learning dances, ultimately performing on the stage at Pride and at the Pride kickoff party.

I was the Operations Director and created the military component of the Pride Board at that time, so it was easy to get us showcased. Our performances went over very well, and St. Charles invited our military element to open their Pride event. Even though St. Louis lost the bid for the OutGames to come here, many good things evolved from that. I knew in my heart this all meant increased awareness, changed perceptions, recognition, and acceptance.

The University of Missouri–St. Louis (UMSL) invited me to speak annually at their Department of Military and Veteran Studies Program. It was a nice way to share my experience with folks who were wondering how it was to serve while not being allowed to be out of the closet. Speaking at these classes, educating the students on diversity and about serving in the military when it wasn't accepted, and the ways I survived and grew, furthered my mission. I spoke at a transgender rally in St. Louis, holding the American flag the whole time to remind everyone in attendance, "This flag is yours too. Don't let anyone tell you that you don't have the same rights and freedoms as they do. If they take issue with it, other countries who don't believe in the American way will take them in."

My time sitting on the parade board as chairman was ending, and I didn't want to run for another four-year term. I felt proud of all I had accomplished, but it was time for me to step down. The mayor at that time approached me and asked me to be a commissioner to the Soldiers Memorial. I graciously accepted and served as a commissioner but only for a year. The term was for two years, but I was having to come to terms with personal family issues.

My public and personal lives were conflicting in major ways, mostly with how I saw myself versus how my family saw and treated me. After a few devastating reality checks, I was basically disowned by my immediate family after I went home to announce I wanted to get married to my then boyfriend. People I knew walked out of the room and didn't talk with me. Having been made to feel unwelcome, we left. Later that evening, I received a text, saying they don't want me around, and if I do come around, I am not allowed to talk about my life and being gay. They thought I was shoving it down their throats. It went on to say how much of an embarrassment I was to the whole family.

This led to me going into a tailspin. I broke up with my boyfriend and I turned on myself. I realized I would never be accepted by people I knew on any level. Despite all my efforts to do the right thing, be a good person—an honorable military man—have people I cared about be proud of me, I realized none of that mattered to them. Fifty-three years of all that torment, marginalization, and pain came at me like a boulder and knocked me off my feet.

This was the beginning of the end—another hard lesson I had to learn for myself and to come to terms with. I started drinking, which resulted in missing days of work. I was also insulted by my boss at the sales job I had, and the stress of it made me walk off the job. The sheer unhappiness of feeling stuck was overwhelming. To top it off, someone I was very close to was diagnosed with a life-threatening illness and no one told me. When I bumped into this person, I could clearly see something was not right, but no one was willing to tell me what was going on. About a year later, I found out it had been cancer and that it, thankfully, had been cured. It seemed the reason no one wanted to tell me the truth was they thought I was too emotional about everything and were concerned that I would have put it all over Facebook, despite my caring and loving nature. I felt it was more about them trying to control things and to try to push me down. They were aware of all my accomplishments, which furthered their prejudice toward me. Jealousy was rampant. I wasn't allowed to talk about anything I had done because it was interpreted as me being better than them. My drinking increased.

A few weeks after I abandoned a job, my car broke down. It was going to cost me $2,500 to get it repaired. This was too much for me. I couldn't bear it. I was already in a bad space and didn't want to deal with it, so I told the dealership where I took the car that it was theirs. I told them that it was outrageous to charge me that much money and that they now owned the car. The only way I could alleviate the stress was to just leave it there. I still owed on it, but I couldn't deal with it anymore.

I had already made the decision to leave to do seasonal work and didn't want to commit to a lease. I was staying with friends because I didn't have my own place and drinking heavily. I'd completely broken off communication with many people I knew because I didn't want to deal with them any longer. Even though I'd accomplished many good things and had been recognized for my accomplishments, they weren't enough. I finally accepted that most of my family never loved or valued me. That was the last bit of rejection I had to face, and though it brought me to my knees, I did accept it.

Dana, Little Mary, and my friend Mary were constantly there for me so I could cry, talk, vent, etc. These women gave of themselves; any time of day or night, they were there for me. They gave me strength, and they always answered my calls. They listened. Their insight and love kept me from spiraling even further down a black hole. Little Mary and Dana knew how I was raised with torment and bigotry, so their insight and support were deeply valued. My friend Mary didn't have that insight but knew from brief encounters what kind of family I came from. I leaned on all three women, as I didn't have the strength to hold myself up. I had to have their help to find love in my heart for myself to get me through this last remnant of painful realization.

20 : What's in Your Heart?

I was losing ground on my psyche, fast.

A friend of mine was dealing with some devastating life challenges in Scotland, so I thought I would travel there to help him out emotionally. Clearly this was misguided because I couldn't face the fact that, once again, I wasn't dealing with my own emotions. What I was going through was coming to a head. I could manage relationships outside my family, but the relationships I had with them and how they treated me remained deeply painful. I had to hit rock bottom to be able to come to terms with it. That's eventually what happened. I couldn't understand then that having my family disown me because of their perceived embarrassment of me was a projection of their own emotional issues.

So, I went to Scotland to be with my friend. I was there for three months. We drank a lot together. I came back home seeking seasonal jobs around the country. I was going through the same old emotional upheaval with how my family saw me and how I saw myself. I was trying to come to terms with the fact that they would never accept or respect the real me. Recognizing the futility of trying to change that was my final stage of release. I didn't know how to come to terms with walking away from all the hate and dysfunction I was receiving from them. I wasted time dwelling on how things could have been versus how they were.

It wasn't just about me being gay. Our beliefs about how to live a quality life were completely opposite. I was heading for a wall with this emotional state of mind. The duality of me being family-oriented and able to have great relationships with so many other people but unable to experience anything except dysfunction from people I knew was tearing me apart. They held me accountable for their unhappiness. I was somehow responsible for their lack of self-esteem. They would accuse me of starting all kinds of problems. The reality was, I would call them out on their lies and be blamed for stirring up shit. I was dealing with people who didn't like themselves, projected it onto me, and I couldn't deflect it. I started sliding into despair and depression and kept drinking pretty heavily. I knew I didn't want to be in St. Louis any longer. So instead of getting a place of my own, I stayed with friends, living in spare rooms or their sofas until seasonal jobs started in a few months. If something doesn't work in my life, I leave it. I am understanding to a point, then after that, I'm done.

Free of obligations, I knew the corporate world was not for me, that being a success was not about earning money. It's about being the best person I can be. I've seen what money does to people, and I didn't want that. People think earning lots of money is being a success. I don't consider it a success in any sense of the word. Being a decent person, making right things happen, and not hurting anyone in the process of living is being a success. If people lead with money, I walk the other way. I think they are damaged and want nothing to do with them. My personality doesn't need money to be strong; it is strong on its own. Excess weakens a person so they don't have to come to terms with who they are. Money provides a facade, not success. My personality, character, and virtues are fine on their own. I wanted to be a success on a more fulfilling and enlightened level, and in the eyes of many others, that's what I had achieved.

I sold many of my things to lighten my load. I filed bankruptcy as I hadn't saved, and the jobs I'd had making lots of money had evaporated. I put what I wanted to keep in storage and set my sights on doing things I loved. I didn't know the term "seasonal work" until I landed a job in that category.

I was in my mid-fifties now but still stuck in family-induced upheaval, questioning everything, avoiding answers by drinking. I wanted to walk away from conventional society, from anything that resembled what society deemed *normal*. I was desperate and floundering, emotionally distraught, so I just disappeared, looking for adventures that weren't available in St. Louis.

I started with the things that pulled on my heart. I like snow skiing, camping, and the mountains. Focusing on those three elements, I started applying for jobs.

In the meantime, I landed a full-time job working at Express Scripts and had a part-time job cleaning two restaurants for Basso and Boundary to earn enough money to get me anywhere but where I was. I would arrive at these restaurants at three in the morning, clean them fully by eight, and go back to where I was staying. I showered and was at Express Scripts by eleven to start my shift and work until eight in the evening. I maintained this schedule for about five months. These restaurants were part of the Cheshire Hotel. Little did I know it at the time, but the Cheshire would become my go-to when I was in town. I made a name for myself, or I should say, my work ethic made a name for me. The general manager knew how hard I worked. Anytime I came back to St. Louis between jobs, I was always welcomed back to work for however long I needed until I left again. I will be forever grateful for him.

In the meantime, I sent an application to Big Sky Ski Resort in Montana for a ticket-checking position. I received a call a few weeks later and an interview was set up. I was hired and set to leave in the middle of November 2018. The season didn't start until November, so I had a few months to save more money. I worked these jobs until I'd earned a healthy savings to get me out to Big Sky.

I worked the entire ski season at Big Sky. Man, did I have a great time. I eventually became a supervisor and ran the morning meetings. I started each day with an uplifting life quote. The twenty-somethings all loved this and loved me. I took them under my wing and led with compassion and care. My supervisor saw my leadership ability and integrity.

I'd also landed a part-time job working at a local restaurant off the mountain washing dishes. Both these jobs were unbelievably satisfying. I loved both. The feelings I felt being in Montana with these wonderful people fill my heart today with warmth and love. These young adults gave me more than they will ever know. They helped me regain some of the family love I had lost for myself—not all, just some. It was enough to put me back on track with my life. I will love all of them forever and will never forget any of them. And I have a beautiful reminder. A book was created for me by one of the folks who worked for me. She made it out of all the old schedules, watering them down to a paste to make paper for the inside of the book where I could write on it. It was stitched together by hand with a beautiful cover. These are the words she inscribed for me in the book, a gift from my entire team:

> Dated 22 April 2019
>
> Steve,
> You worked so hard to make sure all of us at Big Sky had a transformative experience this year (at Big Sky and Beyond). Let this book be a reminder of the friendships made, the Blue Bird days, the agonizingly cold days, the frustrations and the laughs—a physical representation of transformation—holding onto the memories and letting go of things you no longer need.
>
> Much Love, Your Team!

I was brought to tears receiving and then reading this beautiful acknowledgment, Universe-sent, full of love and acceptance. Before I left, I made a video with a soundtrack of memories created there with all of us working the slopes. I am aligned with my role in the Universe and with people. All these gifts throughout my life affirms this. (Many lights were added there.)

I flew back to Scotland after this job ended in April 2019 then came back to the States after three months. I made some nice friends while I was living over there—beautiful souls who are empaths and can see people, who saw me and I saw them. We are still friends and stay in touch.

I started thinking about my life and the way it mattered, not just to me, but others who valued the beautiful parts of me. I still felt compelled to prove to myself that I am valuable and worthy.

21 : Finding the Few

A person doesn't need a lot of people in their lives to help get through struggles; they just need a few really good ones who can be trusted. That's all. I was blessed that throughout my life I had people show up when I needed them the most. I paid attention to who was entering my life and recognized their influence. Some are no longer in my life; some have passed on and some are still with me. All these people I recognized as my lights. Each of them was strong enough to hold me up when I was unable to do so myself. Their love for me was all I needed to get through the struggles intact.

My approach to life is very different from most others. My personality does not allow for the lack of virtues or integrity in others. I am an independent thinker and a solitary creature. The older I get, the more I like being alone. I'm not lonely; there's a difference. I like being away from people for the most part. What I experience and the energy I feel from some people makes me know I don't want to know that person; I can just tell. I want peace in my life, so I don't engage them. I'm happy! I took it upon myself to stay away and not focus on the real reasons why. I wished my choices could have been understood, but they weren't.

I used to be a safe haven for my younger relatives. Now that i see them as adults, they seem unable to live and let live; they haven't learned from the experiences of others and a few have continued to adopt the same-old family opinions and judgments. They think I should still come around, ignoring the boundaries I have set for myself. Since I lived my life completely opposite from everyone they know, an attribute that at one time they had respected in me, they'd decided they could no longer separate themselves from the bias that surrounds them.

Along with control, the other thing that takes place is withholding information, which comes across as a power move. I found out after the fact that my family had withheld some very serious, vital health information from me because they didn't want me to get emotional. "So, you still think having emotions is a weakness in people," I asked, "and especially me because of being gay?"

I continued to get confirmation that I was seen as weak and emotional by my family affected me deeply. I thought I'd learned to live with it, but I realized what I'd been doing was suppressing it. It was the pressure of conflicting views that led me to drink to numb the pain and leave to remove myself from it.

The drinking took me down. By this point, I'd stopped going around for holidays for about four years to avoid the torment. It was a vicious cycle because others would start arguing with me, and of course, I would defend myself, which was looked at as not getting along. Manipulation at its finest.

The course in personal development I took taught me to stay away from dysfunction and negative energy, so I stayed true to that, but there was still so much emotional turmoil inside that I wasn't dealing with effectively. I finally realized that although I didn't see myself as a drinker, I was drinking more than ever before. I knew that wasn't for me, but here I was, free, living on my terms, and trying desperately to leave the pain from the past. It was tough. I am genuinely family-oriented, so I was waging a perpetual inner battle. I had a lot more work to do to get and remain in touch with myself.

By September, I was still staying with friends and bouncing from home to home and couch to couch doing odd jobs while also working as a houseman for that boutique hotel in St. Louis. All the jobs I landed provided amazing freedom. I had no responsibility other than the job at hand. I could come and go and not be stressed. I was living a life free of worry.

It was time to look for another seasonal job. This time I thought it would be cool to live on the beach, so I focused my energy on finding a job that enabled me to do that. I found one on Captiva Island, off the coast of southern Florida west of Fort Myers, working for a company that rents bikes and wave runners and offers parasailing trips and all sorts of ocean and water thrill-seeking entertainment. I drove to Captiva in November, got situated, and never missed a day of work. I was, however, hungover a lot of the time, and I'd started smoking cigarettes while drinking.

One night, after drinking, I went to bed and had a dream. In my dream, my friend Jeff, who passed a year prior, my Aunt (Big) Mary, who passed six months prior, and a beautiful girl with long brown hair all came to visit me in my dream. Aunt Mary said, "You have to stop doing this to yourself. There is much more waiting for you." Jeff was dancing around with a white piece of paper in the back pocket of his jeans. He pulled it out and sort of waved it and then looked at it. I didn't know what it was. I then asked who the beautiful girl was.

She said, "I am your Guardian Angel." I asked her name. "You will know me as Marie Antoinette." She had long brown hair and wore a white blouse tucked into a long brown skirt.

I turned to my Aunt Mary and asked, "Is Dad there?"

She said, "Yes."

"Can I speak with him?" I asked.

"It is not time for you to do that."

I woke up from that dream, wild-eyed and shaken. That dream is as vivid to me now as it was when it happened. Even writing this, I can see each detail. That dream made me stop drinking and smoking. I tossed any remaining items out.

It was the end of January 2020. I quit my beach job, drove back to St. Louis, and started working on repairing the damage to my well-being. I determined I was finally discarding my family and any semblance of acceptance from them. It was the hardest action I've ever faced. Back to St. Louis, I went back to work at the boutique hotel to put the final pieces of myself back together. My life took on a different meaning due to that awakening of the dream. I finally felt I had accepted the fact that I was free of my family dysfunction. I literally felt I had saved myself from death, which, along with other valuable messages, that dream was telling me. I paid attention to it.

I started reading and talking more with my confidants, Dana, Mary, and Little Mary—the people I trusted, people whose thinking and behaviors were healthy. Mostly I stayed to myself, camping alone, regrouping my psyche, as I had done at different times in my life. The most important thing I did was take stock of my virtues, how I treated people, how they responded to me, and what I've contributed. I noted all the things I'd done to bring awareness and public consciousness to the LGBTQIA+ community. All of the aspects of my personality allowed me to bring to fruition the beautiful life I had created for myself and others. I know I am a beautiful human. Being gay is one component of what makes me "me." I think it is one of my best features, along with paying attention to other people and receiving what they send to me. Some might call it validation. I called it "psyche food."

Cousin Dana and Steve, 2018.

Reaching out to talk with Little Mary, Dana, and my friend Mary was invaluable, beyond words. They helped me take credit for what I've done and who I was. They kept me thriving and growing. I feel proud that I leave good impressions on people and share with them the best parts of my being. I want them to feel good and know they matter. This has always been me.

Aunt Mary, my cousin Dana, and my friend Mary are selfless women who loved me unconditionally and helped me stay true to myself. A few of my aunts and cousins helped me believe in myself when I was tormented at a young age. There were many times I felt as if I couldn't breathe. For twenty-six years, my friend Mary listened to me complain about the way my family treated me. She was there when I had breakups and breakdowns. My Aunt Mary and cousin Dana have been with me my whole life. They know me for the person I am. Because of these three strong women, I found solid footing and was able to build strength and confidence in myself. May the Universe always watch over them and my other lights for always being there for me with their strength and resolve. They are among the few that held me up.

I finally understood that there was a profound sadness behind my drinking; it kept me from accepting that I may never have people in my life who are accepting and love me unconditionally. It was the last remnant I was trying to come to terms with during my brief drinking phase. It was tough to accept and hard to let go of the illusion.

I am beyond this now, although it wasn't easy. It meant having to adjust my thinking. It meant visiting my mom on my terms and avoiding contact with the rest of the family. I am free of the torment; more importantly, I am free to be me on all levels and not worry about what others think.

Steve and Little Mary, 2015.

22 : Lessons Learned

My mission is to get and stay in touch with my soul.

I've learned a lot from living my life, writing my story, and reading what I've written. I've been asked to share and document what I've experienced, which is the reason for this book. The lessons I've learned are pretty powerful for me, and I hope will be a force for others to identify with and then live powerful lives too.

It is important to pay attention to the people who come to you at a time when *you* need strength. If they can't give you what you need, do the right thing for yourself. Your values, integrity, and character will always be tested by people coming to you.

Be careful with how you are asked to show up for them. Rely on your own strength of character and what you want to manifest, but also lean on people you trust for support to get to the next level of yourself. It will be hard, but you can do it. I did it!

When it comes to understanding yourself, it's almost impossible to know or accept what needs to be done if your mind is filled with untruths: those you've been told and the ones you tell yourself. My mind was always filled with thoughts about family that may have been true and some that seemed to have happened but didn't. Look at the situation with the facts alone. That's enough. No embellishment needed.

Don't allow your mind to turn on yourself; stop any self-inflicted terrorist attack. Let reason fill your mental space. Accept and move on, leaving dysfunction behind.

Stop chasing acceptance, love, and respect. Be accepting, loving, and respectful of yourself, and these things will come to you.

 Understand that humans have a primal need to be loved, and that our first opportunity to encounter love unconditionally is with family. This is where the pain can come from, that place where unconditional love should have existed but wasn't provided. In reality, the only love that matters is the love you have for yourself. That was my most enlightened awakening.

Believe in yourself. Rely on yourself. Stay strong, relying on your own strength to be the best you can be. This is about as powerful as a human can be with themselves. You have to remove yourself from unhealthy situations. Stay by yourself; be alone to figure things out. Many answers surface when you are silent and disengaged from everything.

Let nature give you peace and joy: sounds, smells, a waft of a breeze, a leaf falling or growing green. Nature offers respite.

Dig deep inside yourself to the core of who you are. Stay there until you have the strength to be your best self.

Enjoy your life, make it work for you; no time is better or worse than the current moment. It's up to you and how you look at it.

We all have the opportunity to learn and grow each day, and every moment, to prove what we are made of. Pay particular attention to what comes to you, what the Universe sends to guide you or change your path. Be ever cognizant of this. Once you get through your hard times in life, use your power, energy, your gifts to manifest your passions to leave a lasting memory with a better world of awareness for all. Believe me, it matters not just to you but to everyone you reach.

23 : Unencumbered

I'm a strong, kind, loving, sexy man.

In the fall of 2021, I returned to St. Louis for a few months and stayed with friends. The beauty was I didn't have to pay them to stay with them. I just did odd things around their homes to earn my keep. Now that I have my military pension and benefits, it was good not having to dip into my savings except for food and gas and insurance for the car. I used to drive BMWs. Now I drive a 2006 four-door Chevy Cobalt. It was cheap, I paid cash for it, and it's all I need. I love it.

Continuing to do seasonal work, I landed one of my favorite jobs at Grand Teton National Park as a houseman at Flagg Ranch. I was outside all the time, going to each of the cabins that dotted the top of the mountain resort. I would drive the golf cart to replenish the linen closets so the housekeepers could clean the rooms and make them ready for the next occupants. The setting was beautiful. I saw deer daily. Chipmunks and all sorts of wildlife would stroll through the cabins. A squirrel hopped in my golf cart to see what candy he or she could take. Occasionally, a grizzly bear would appear. We were all equipped with bear spray just in case. Thankfully, none of us had to use it. On my days off, a few of us would drive to the mountains for a day hike. The scenery was breathtaking. Just being in the wilderness like that, breathing the clean air and hiking next to cliffs, on the edge of the trail looking down at trees, valleys, and lakes, was like being in a scene out of a movie. I made some good friends (lights) there too.

I returned to St. Louis a little earlier than planned, as there was another health issue in my family. This time, I got involved because it was something that she couldn't have done for herself. She couldn't be alone, and I had the flexibility to stay with her. It worked out great. She did well, and perhaps for the first time, I had a clear, unattached perspective on how I was being treated.

In my mind, when crises happen, it is supposed to bring people closer together. I wasn't sure how long I would need to be in St. Louis, so I rented an apartment for a year. I was at peace coming home to help her. I didn't care how long it took; I wanted to make sure she was going to be OK before I left again. As the saying goes, *there is no greater honor than to take care of the ones who once took care of you.* Without question, regardless of how my I'm treated, I will always be there for people.

The year-long lease was set to end in 2022. I've been looking for a van to live in so I can continue to do seasonal work. I Googled seasonal work in St. Louis, figuring since I am staying here for the time being, I might as well do something. I applied for a job at Forest Park Forever, working in the Nature Reserve. I was called to come in for an interview. This was in December 2021. The interview went well, and I received a call saying they wanted to hire me. I was excited, as this job was working outside 99 percent of the time. I started work after the first of the year. My first day was really nice. We sat in the dayroom with all these other people, but I didn't know who I would actually be working with until the meeting ended. That's when Catherine came up to me and said, "You're going to be working with me, Kevin, and Israel."

I met Kevin and knew instantly that he and Catherine were really nice people. I met Israel, who was on vacation, the following Monday. It took no time at all to realize this job would be especially satisfying because of the people I would be working with, outside, in Forest Park. This was the perfect job for me. All the people have great personalities coupled with their working knowledge for their specific work zones.

As time went on, and I really got to know these people on more personal levels, it dawned on me how wonderful these people really were. That's when it sank in. When I am around people who are looking for the best in life, themselves, and others, my personality fits right in with them. They recognized these traits in me as well. The working relationships we cultivated are relationships I will always keep with me. All these people are lights in my meadow now. These people have become lifelong friends, and I am grateful for their friendships and that they want to keep me as a friend too. They were all full-time employees, and as a seasonal worker, I was a bit of an outsider. That status separation melted away and I became one of them. The goodness in each of us was shining brighter, and we enjoyed one another's company. Every day I looked forward to coming to work to see all these people, especially my team.

24 : The Signs

I always paid attention to signs as they came to me. I was and still am observant, perhaps to a fault. I like being alone, but I'm not lonely; I just like my solitude. This is an inherited trait from my mom. I know what is going on and can see what is happening before people realize it for themselves. I don't know if I engineered that sense or if it was an innate quality, but I am glad I have it.

Even as a kid, I knew I was nice and had a big heart. I protected that heart even when it was being hurt all the time. I guarded it. When I discovered that people willingly and deliberately tried to hurt one another, just because they could, it was profoundly upsetting. I knew it was shameful and spoke volumes about who they really were, with their lack of empathy or kindness. My family always thought I brought shame to them. I have sadness for the lives they have lived.

Which brings me to the kind of life I am living and how, just by being myself, I am able to make people feel comfortable in my presence, to the point they open up about themselves and share what they are feeling. I seem to have a unique insight for helping people explore and discover their own worth. I'm grateful that so many I've helped were able to reach the next level in their career or life. I've learned that I have a way of giving people permission to take risks, and when they do, they appreciate it. Affecting people in a positive way is what I am most proud of.

Every accomplishment I have achieved has been the result of my creative outlook, backed by a massive amount of sentiment. What motivates me is sharing experiences and turning them into good memories.

I used to seek validation for things that I have accomplished because I needed others to be proud of who I was and what I'd done. I liked being noticed for the good I offered the world. At the worst of times growing up, I knew without a doubt that I would make a difference in the lives of people and leave my gentle mark on this world. The strength I gained when life did not serve me well is something I have relied on as I have become my own person, living my life on my terms.

Over time and with exposure, I realized everyone struggles with their identity and insecurities, but gay people struggle with having their identities accepted. Many labor to gain their own voice, mostly on their own, without support from their family, churches, schools, or other social backdrops. Some gay youth never make it to adulthood because of others making them feel ashamed of who they are. Others reach adulthood and develop addictions to keep the pain from surfacing because they don't know how to process the pain inflicted on them. The most important thing I've learned is to be honest with all of it and shun the people who can't accept others' differences. I've also learned that gay people are very observant and attuned to others. This is how we survive.

I gained emotional intelligence from the trauma caused by abuse. Being marginalized, humiliated, left out, and made to feel like I wasn't worth loving by people who were supposed to love me unconditionally was emotionally damaging! How could I expect anyone else to do anything different? I observed these people going to church after making someone feel bad for simply being who they were, as if church would make it all proper and acceptable. That is hypocritical. It's especially terrible when mean, insecure adults have kids and then turn their kids into bullies. It's unbelievable to me that they haven't learned anything from or about life at their ages. My advice: Stay away from bullies and negativity.

I am an activist now, with a very strong voice. I am aware of my strengths, abilities, compassion, empathy, understanding, and accomplishments. I've gained an incredible amount of confidence from all the things I have done and been through in my life to reach my higher self. I stand for people who don't have their own voice yet and let them know they matter too. I also let the bullies of our society know that they won't get away with intimidation. If they want to show support, that is cool, but they can't belittle or make people who are not like them feel they don't have a right to be here. If they try to, I give them a list of countries that will take them—countries without freedom or respect for humanity. My military background pushed that forward for me.

I'm glad that times have changed and continue to change. Things and people where I grew up are not like they were. Today, people, including many members of my extended family, see me as Steve, a nice guy who is kind.

As I look back on my life and what I have given to myself, I am pleased. My innate qualities have shown through the entire time. There were many times that I hid them growing up, but they were still there. I am proud of how I am living and have lived. I have a few regrets here and there, but never to the point of me being ashamed of the way I lived my life. My beautiful qualities stand on their own. I have apologized to people I've hurt—the legitimate hurt of a lie or making someone feel bad for breaking up with me. I know that people see my heart and my welcoming smile. I've had people ask how I have survived life intact. My answer to that question is, "I left when I was nineteen." I feel proud of how I'm able to answer that question, which is the essence of this book. People were placed in my path by the Universe to help me grow. Now, when I meditate and become one with the Universe, I speak to the Universe and ask for guidance, signs, or validation for certain things. Inevitably, what I ask for appears. I embrace and explore my being to find what lies deep within me and then I bring it into my life. I am not religious or traditional in any sense of the word. I believe in the ancient beliefs of the Norse Gods. It turns out, according to my DNA results, I have way more Norse blood than German. I was pleasantly surprised as I thought I was more German. Being a survivor and a warrior are primal for me; these attributes are deep in my DNA. I feel at peace. I am home with my Norse heritage and beliefs. I don't believe in man-made, orga-nized faiths that teach people to hate themselves and/or each other.

I've learned on my own, and having discovered this interesting fact about me, I am immersed in that culture and beliefs. I have officiated a wedding, a funeral, and a few healings. I am developing my sense of mysticism and feel it is my calling to become a shaman in this realm of spirituality. In Viking tradition, the shamans were female and called Völva. I am currently in the learning phases of this and will take it into higher levels of thinking. I will not be told how to live or what to believe. I respect the laws of nature. Why would I have to be told how to be a good person?

I love myself. That is what I finally realized. It was hard to hold onto this when most everyone in my background told me I was damaged. But I did realize it, and glimmers of it stayed even though I had a fleeting thought of ending my life back in those days. Staying true to who I am paid off in so many ways. Each trip around the sun was worth it to get me to where I am now. I have had beautiful people come into my life and leave the most precious gifts with me. These are the people who matter. Money can't provide such gifts. Words, expressions of gratitude, love, and kindness have all been shared with and expressed to me. When all is said and done, I just hope people remember me as someone who cared, made a difference, and who they could call a friend.

The only things that I can take with me when I pass on is what's in my heart and soul. I matter. And I can say with pride that I have never made anyone feel like people have made me feel growing up and into my adulthood. I have faults. I have my own way of looking at life, and I live life on my terms. I take time when I need it. I fall off the radar and regroup. But nothing can make me treat others like they don't matter or don't have value. I know I bring goodness, warmth, compassion, and understanding into my relationships, my work teams, my life—all mixed with kindness and love. Thank goodness, I didn't learn to be cruel by being treated cruelly.

I am still—and will always be—a work in progress. There is much I have to learn, achievements I hope to accomplish, beauty I want to create. Instead of using my energy to cope with and understand my past, I now focus fully on helping myself and others become their best selves while enlightening my mental well-being because, first, I must know myself. I need to know and understand who I am and what makes my personality stand out in the world. I know and understand my past fully enough to know to leave it out of my present and future. It is no longer relevant because how I look at myself is much more powerful than how I was seen.

We are each alone in this world. No one can give another what they need or understand truly what they are going through, but we can provide support, empathy, and, hardest of all, unconditional love. To move into the different depths of my being, I meditate, take walks, and let my mind flow where it wants. I hold myself accountable through my pen, which is the healthiest way for me to stay honest with life. I think before I speak, using my unending humor, which I inherited from my dad, to touch people in a very profound and loving way.

I have discovered I can write anytime, anywhere. I can easily put my mind at ease and embody the calming solitude I seek. I have written on the coast of Denmark sitting on the North Sea, also known as the German Ocean. I have camped in the Scottish Highlands at Loch Awe and throughout Europe. I've visited places that first came to me in dreams or in books, then I made them a reality.

Recently, I have twice chosen to write in the area where I grew up: Trappers Fall, Prairie du Rocher, Illinois. The energy I feel there, from generations of my people, is as familiar as Mom's cooking. Tapping into that energy, my words flow as never before. The familiar sounds of a far-off train whistle and the wind rustling the leaves are gentle reminders of days gone by. I remain alone as complete darkness envelops me. I hear the trees crack, a few wild animals foraging, all parts of this unique experience. These sounds have special meaning because, as a child, I took comfort hearing them and knowing my forefathers heard the same sounds long ago.

Surrounded by forest, this place is nestled between bluffs, with a clearing big enough to hold a few lakes with a few homes, campers, and cabins, far enough removed to not disturb the wilderness aspect. The owners of this property know my family. Barbie is the current proprietor of this place. Her spirit is one with the area. She embodies the characteristics of the area she manages. Her warmth, natural beauty, kindness, and gentle spirit are one with the nature that surrounds her, and being with her makes me feel I've known her my whole life. That's a feeling that isn't embodied in many people. Her father and mother had a vision that became this camping and fishing area. The first time I camped here was in a tent; this time, I'm in a cabin. This wild, natural space gives me a sense of oneness with the Universe. The tranquility and peace I feel are like being a character in one of Henry David Thoreau's books. I am able to get into my thoughts and have the words flow. I'm able to delve into myself to find the right meaning to convey what I am feeling, reflecting all that surrounds me. Hearing a fire crackling, feeling its warmth, and watching the billowing smoke is comforting and primal, an instinct in which there is something familiar but still foreign. It's the best of both worlds: being wild, natural and yet close to the modern conveniences we have today. I'm not entirely alone. Copper, the dog, spends time with me, his presence adding to the atmosphere of peace. I like having him visit me, spending time around the fire.

Trappers Fall is right here, in my backyard, so to speak. I am in a peaceful mindset with a distinct difference. This place is familiar; it's where I grew up. Drawing inspiration from this is even natural. The whole area speaks to me, as if through the wind. Even though it doesn't really matter which setting I choose to write, with all places providing the energy my mind needs to put emotion to paper, this place is different. Even with all the places I've been in the United Kingdom, Europe, and the United States, Trappers Fall offers a resolution to my conflicted feelings: never wanting to go back to where I grew up because of painful memories and attitudes, and desperately needing to go back "home." To my surprise, I find comfort here and can draw on heartaches and memories as the inspiration for this book. What I find fascinating is that I left home, never wanting to return, wanting to escape to distant lands as far away from the resentment and disdain as I could. Yet, here I am, finding solace in the very area I was escaping.

Embracing this is cathartic. If it weren't for my past, I wouldn't be able to write this book in the first place. I listened to my intuition when I took a good hard look at the sign outside this area. I knew it was a place I wanted to explore to find out what feelings and emotions I would gain from it. So, I called and was allowed to pitch a tent, even though that usually wasn't allowed, because the owner knows me. I took a chance. I am allowing the peace within me to just be. A surprising congruency has been established in my psyche because of making this choice. I will be returning to this place, not just for the beauty it holds, but for the beauty it has given me.

25 : Becoming an Enlightened Thinker

The only way to be completely honest about life, and live a healthy, enlightened one, is to take accountability for your faults and stop holding others accountable for your behavior.

Working on myself has led to many wonderful discoveries. I read Voltaire, John Locke, and a few other enlightened thinkers. I started reading their works a few years ago and discovered that their way of thinking was much like mine, so I adopted it into my lifestyle. Then I realized I had started my enlightened journey when I was a child, as their philosophies mirrored the ones I had already thought of back in the day. These discoveries validated my thinking, my way of seeing the world. I'm an independent thinker with enough strength and courage to live the way I think and feel. I love being in my own company. I have survived and thrived. I knew at an early age that I liked who I was. I was being shown everywhere what not to be. Now I know I can only do one thing perfectly, and that is to be me. I am content and pleased with the way I made things happen and that I stayed true to myself all the way through.

Being gay is being true to myself, and I've discovered that everyone benefits from having gay people in their lives. In some ancient cultures, gay people were revered; they were looked upon as having two spirits, both male and female. Gays have compassion, understanding, and can help in so many areas where others are afraid to venture. There may be jealousy on both sides, if the men are insecure in their own personalities. Some women are jealous because they desire some gay men, but they like us, and even love us, knowing nothing will come of it.

Many years ago, I was watching an old episode of *Bewitched*. Endora, played by Agnes Moorehead, delivers a line, describing to Samantha, played by Elizabeth Montgomery, about who they are: *I am quicksilver, a fleeting shadow, or a distant sound. My home has no boundaries beyond which I cannot pass. I live in music, in a flash of color. I live on the wind and in the sparkle of a star.* This description felt as if it fit me as well and affirmed that I have always vibrated at a higher frequency than most. The Universe is my home. Where my mind thinks, I go. My opportunities are as limitless as my heart so desires. I am a free thinker, spirit, and human with good intentions. I embody this statement and have adopted it into my being.

The military gave me a lot, but the most important thing was confidence in myself to be all I want, to have the courage to recognize opportunities, and then to act on them to make them a reality. That confidence enabled me to take risks and be accountable for my actions. Among many things, it helped me to expand my already natural abilities and virtues to their full potential.

I have a good heart. I like my kindness and gentle nature. I like how I love people, whether it is returned or not. I like that I can see the goodness in life and in people. I stay away from people who harbor meanness, nastiness, and ugliness. Brave, generous, witty, friendly, spirited, benevolent, industrious, conscientious, self-reliant, and disciplined are a few virtues I am most noted for having and what I look for in others.

I have had so many wonderful things happen to me along the way. The Universe reminds and rewards me for the goodness I bring to life here on earth. My dear Aunt Joyce, who was married to my godfather. made angels for people out of beads. She gave me one at a wedding once, before she passed on. I was probably forty-eight when she gave it to me. I remember her saying, "I think you are an angel here on this earth." Her husband was there and heard her say this to me. It moved me, and although I was speechless, I did manage to tell her "Thank you." Wherever I go, I take that little angel with me.

I knew who I was and that being a boy growing into a man was way more than the gender itself. To me, being a man goes much deeper than not showing emotion, sleeping with a girl and having kids, or joining the military, hunting, etc. Being a man is to be strong, able to show empathy and vulnerability, process emotions, show weakness, and admit mistakes. Most importantly, being a man means holding himself accountable with integrity while accepting he can falter sometimes, like the rest of us. My dad was a man. In the rural area where I grew up, the ideal man is rugged, gets drunk, has sex with women, is opinionated and judgmental, with an ego that overtakes every part of his being. They are expected to be assholes. However, picking on physically or emotionally weaker people does not make anyone a man.

I attribute some of my success to the military giving me the strength and resolve to support my existing virtues and character to the best of my ability. My nature, my DNA, guides me to be the best person possible, to be strong enough to survive, intact, and share the essence of what I've gained.

The other part of that success is my own will to survive. Most of my success as a human comes from how I think and the way I approach life. The military gave me the confidence in myself to survive and then thrive. When I started first grade, I was scared and timid. The teacher had my mom wait in the hallway until I calmed down. She gave me three pieces of Play-Doh and said, in her gentle way, you sit here and play with this until you feel comfortable to go meet the other kids. I did that, and it helped.

Here's my advice: You have to start somewhere; why not at the basic level of who and what you are? Protect your essence at all costs, without hurting others. Be quiet if you need to be. This is the most important thing. Pay attention to the Universe and what opportunities are sent your way; filter through what you think will be good for you, not just your heart and hormones, but also your mind and soul.

I aligned myself with strong, free-thinking people throughout my life, did a great job, and only let on that I was gay when it was reasonable to do so.

I took advantage of the guidance and reassurance I received. I finally learned to celebrate who I was.

I am a beautiful mix of both my parents, but I am the living legacy of my dad. I am more like my father than I thought I was. I didn't realize this until I got older. Aside from the farming aspect, he and I shared the same generous, thoughtful, kind heart, which is the source of everything good. I will never be as accomplished as Dad was as a farmer, mechanic, or have an eye for beautiful cars. I received a gift from him which came to me in a different way—by being able to reach out and touch people in a profound way, seeking and seeing beauty wherever I go. He is in my heart, as is his kindness, humility, and ability to help others with compassion and love. His sense of humor is within me too. Ask anyone who has ever worked with or dated me, I am a practical joker. My dad would have loved all this in me. I was fortunate enough to get the strengths of his inner being. Being gay is such a small fraction of who I am. I stand up for what's right; I am a voice for those who feel they can't speak or aren't strong enough to do so against injustices. I make people mad when I stand up for the rights of others—just ask my family. I will do what's correct, regardless of what anyone else thinks. This was also in my dad's personality. I am passionate about fairness and keeping things fair. My parents both had strong work ethics. I was fortunate enough to inherit this from them. I inherited my mother's strength, solitary nature, steadfastness, desire to be independent, and adventure-seeking. That strength is what helped me survive growing up and many times in my adult life as well.

My mom and dad live on in me. I feel it and I know it. Their "information streams" are not lost in the Universe, per a law of quantum physics. I find this to be a very positive and hopeful statement. My nature, as was my dad's, is to be helpful, to find goodness in people. I didn't want to disappoint anyone, but people let me know whenever I did. Now, when I walk into a room, I bring in the undeniable energy of optimism, and my light shines brightly. This can feel quite intimidating to those who are narcissists or emotionally inept. Emotional issues cannot hide; they show themselves very quickly.

I needed to have friends when I was younger to develop my socialization and be accepted, or so I was told. My sensitivity was years ahead of my peers at that time. A lot was taken from me early on. I lacked confidence in myself. I have that confidence now and realize I never really needed all that superficial acceptance and validation. As long as I believe in myself, that's all I need. These are lessons my soul had to learn. I was a good kid who became an upstanding, successful man. I have accomplished important things in my life and am proud of these accomplishments. I am distinctly proud of the way I love who I am and hold myself accountable for what I do in life, both good and bad. I think that loving yourself is where life really begins.

Growing up, I didn't truly know what loving myself was; all I knew was that I liked who my inner being was. People projected their beliefs and fears on me, their bias and contempt for anyone who wasn't like them. I believed them until I got much older and realized those fears and beliefs weren't about me.

Sitting at the top of my tree helped me gain perspective many times, but my life truly started when I left home. That is something else that holds its own power. I had to leave everything I knew so that I could grow into the man I am supposed to be. If I'd stayed in the place where I grew up, my growth would have been stunted, and I would have been left in a box. Growing up and marrying the same people you've known since you were old enough to remember did not appeal to me. Instead, I got away to see the world I so desperately yearned for and meet people who I was supposed to meet along the way, each of whom left bits of themselves with me and I with them. I left out of desperation and would not have had that happen any other way. Once I got away, the fear of the unknown quickly changed to curiosity and exploration. I need to be one with my Universe and see everything I can see in my lifetime on this earth and the beauty it holds, including all types of people.

I am always fine on my own. Being alone builds strength. I don't allow anyone to bring me down. My energy stands for itself; people see and feel it. They can sense that I am happy and content not being like other people and not having to fit into a mold. I am just happy with myself and how I live my life and am grateful I've been able to develop meaningful friendships along the way.

Some of the strategies and techniques I use to achieve and maintain a peaceful, loving life include giving myself affirmations every morning in the mirror by saying, "I love you" or "you look great," or "there is no one else you need to impress except you." I like who is looking back at me. I have never intentionally hurt people in the process of living my life; although there were a few times when I may not have handled the situation the best that I could have, partly because I wasn't in an emotionally healthy state of mind at the time, I apologize. I move on. Things do happen; one can't be spot-on all the time, so if you do stumble, apologize. If the other person doesn't accept it, that's on them.

As is obvious in the title of this book, My Lights are the most resonating part of my life. Each person who became one of my lights is still there. Conversely, I am there for each of them too.

Health is extremely important. I pay attention to eating healthy foods and exercising, maintaining my body and health. I can't eat or live like I did when I was in my twenties, thirties, or even fifties. I have to live and nourish my body differently as I approach sixty, always keeping my health in mind.

My mental well-being is healthy and nurtured. Little Mary, Dana, and my friend Mary, all of whom I have mentioned throughout this book, have helped keep me on track, especially if I'm teetering a bit. They are the strongest sounding board of my life. We keep each other balanced at different times.

I will continue my life of explorations, gaining new friends and experiences along the way. I love this. It only matters to me how I feel about myself. We are all interstellar travelers having a human experience. Let's make the best of our journey and enjoy it.

I look at life as a football field: there are the players and there are the spectators on the sidelines. My advice: stay off the sidelines; get on the field and play. It's the only way you'll discover what you are made of and who you are. Take risks, get out of your comfort zone. If you stumble and fail, so what? Get up and try again. Life is to be lived, not observed. Feel it, experience it, and LIVE. You can quote me on this: "Before you know it, your life will be over. You'll want to say you did it, whatever IT is."

I realize more and more how truly happy I am. Out of all the years I have been on this earth, I can take stock and be grateful. I am in a good place mentally. I am happy with who I am and have become. The Universe sends me signs all the time that I am "right on" with my thinking and how I live. Growing up, I always thought I needed people to be around as my friends. But the Universe let me know that by not having them as friends, I could see they weren't good for me. I have good people scattered throughout my life. Now, I am completely satisfied and at peace being alone. I love meeting new people and making friends, and will continue to do so, but it is my nature to be alone and live life on my terms, reaching out occasionally to say hello. Throughout my life, my lights helped me realize I add value just by being present. I will be forever grateful to them for that.

I am immediately uncomfortable around anyone who is negative, without virtues, or who treats people or society badly. I recognize their false energy quickly and steer clear of it. I no longer take things personally, as most things have nothing to do with me. It's usually a projection of the other person.

Freedom, to me, is the example I live by being a loner, being gay, being me, unaltered by the prejudice and opinions of others. Girls love me, many guys do too, and appreciate having a gay person in their lives. From my perspective, being gay means bringing beauty and a freer way of thinking about life. This freedom helps everyone involved.

I am moving more and more into the enlightenment phase of my thinking. My path and my psyche are evolving. I don't do New Year's resolutions. I try to be the best person I can be to myself and others all year round.

The year 2022 has been amazing for me. As I turned sixty in 2022, I asked myself, "What have you learned about yourself and about life up to this point?" I've learned a lot:

- Love who you are and become more loving as you grow and learn.
- Don't follow the crowd, especially if they go against your virtues and character and what you feel is right.
- It's OK to stand alone and take risks.
- Stay away from hate, divisiveness, bigotry, and greed; these are character breakers.
- Be consistent with compassion.
- Always maintain a sense of humor.

- This IS life. Stay flexible and move with it.
- Without doubts and with all the strength in your being, never let anyone or anything hold you back and diminish the love and confidence you have for your ability and potential.
- Pay attention to the signs coming your way. If something bad happens, look at it as a possibility to shift your thinking or the direction of your life.
- If there is one thing that is consistent, it's change. Roll with it until you can establish solid footing based on your emotional intelligence and confidence in yourself.
- Seek enriching life experiences.
- Don't take anything personally. This is the key.
- Accept yourself and make life beautiful.

Here's how I see it for myself. I love making others and myself laugh. Seasonal work around the United States and Europe is a huge part of my life. I will be continuing these adventures. I am constantly striving to do the right thing, for myself and others, but live a solitary life and enjoy the peace that comes with that. Being fair-minded is a major aspect I love about me. Kindness and compassion define me, but I'm not a pushover (weak) and will stand up for what is right. I've learned to be more patient and understanding with myself and others while standing my ground. Peace, harmony, love, and thoughtfulness are the characteristics I strive to maintain on my journey through life. Independence from social norms is liberating. I'm gay, and that's normal for me. I like thinking it's nature's way of providing population control. I value my strength of character.

I was born into the family I was born into, served honorably in the military, and was a member of the Class of 1980, but I don't belong to any of these categories. I belong to the Universe. I'm simply passing through until the next journey presents itself. I define myself. I endeavor to create good energy before I move on. If good vibes were not left behind, for whatever reason, it wasn't intentional.

One of the things I could never wrap my mind around was the notion that we all have to look, act, and be the same. I don't get it, and I stay away from anyone who thinks like this. I mean, I'm not fitting into anyone's idea of who I am except my own.

Enlightened thinking and being secure in oneself paves a lot of brave new paths and lights many a meadow. Today, I can humbly say my meadow is full of lights, each of them representing support and strength that held me up. Each light, each person's unbiased belief in goodness, helped me believe in myself. Their actions taught me how to appreciate what friendship truly is. I will always be especially grateful for the early lights in my life because of the dark times when my own light was extinguished. Those early lights helped me stay alive and become the man I am today.

I still face struggles and challenges. My family still withholds from me, but I am older now, wiser, and understand them and myself better all the time. I stand on a solid foundation, meet challenges head-on, and make decisions based on who I am and what I want to manifest with the emotional intelligence I've gained throughout my life. Life is always exciting with new turns and twists. The phrase "blood is thicker than water" is lost on me. My friends and some family members are thicker than water; some family members are just water. My chosen family is thick. They accept me for who I am.

It has taken me a long time to appreciate who I am and what life means to me. But I have, and I love myself even more for it. What I manifest is what comes to me. I have downsized and gotten rid of everything that I didn't have a sincere connection to and am currently looking for a van that I can live in to travel around doing seasonal work. I am not a follower in any sense of the word. I lead with my heart, with all my senses alert. To me, this is another level of complete freedom. Shifting to further change is a constant in my life. I look forward to times when this happens, as it always takes me in a direction I am supposed to go. I've needed every trip around the sun, believe me. I trust the Universe.

Throughout all the years and positions I've held in the LGBTQIA+ community and other organizations, Steven Louis Brawley, the LGBTQIA+ historian for the St. Louis region, has been documenting what I have done. He added a story about my first wreath-laying ceremony at Soldiers Memorial to the St. Louis LGBTQIA+ History website and documented the seven "firsts" I accomplished. It is all now part of the history of St. Louis's LGBTQIA+ community. Taking things one step further, he initiated the Missouri History Museum's inclusion of my life's work in their LGBTQIA+ archival collection.

The result of all my activism and the realization of me serving as a gay man has led to the Museum's exhibit, which includes the downtown Soldiers Memorial, to permanently preserve my artifacts and documents for future exhibits and research. This will be a permanent exhibit shared between the Missouri History Museum and the Soldiers Memorial. The History Museum has the original flags I carried in the Pride parades, a uniform of mine, papers, and other memorabilia.

The seven firsts I did for our community, our city, and our nation are:

- The wreath-laying ceremony for LGBTQIA+ veterans who gave their life
- Military walking in the Pride parade
- Being commissioner to the Soldiers Memorial
- Walking in the Veterans Day Parade
- Chairman of the board for the Veterans Day Parade
- Bringing Pride to Scott AFB then speaking to the crowd on stage about the importance of having Pride at Diversity Day
- Lighting the Soldiers Memorial in Pride colors, which led to the Civil Courts building being lit in Pride colors too

By creating these firsts, doors were opened for others to get involved and feel more secure with themselves to come out and embrace who they are. This sums up why I do this. I was held back. I was made to feel worthless. I know what that does to the spirit and will not allow that to continue happening to anyone wherever I am in this world. Everyone has a voice, and I will help them realize that.

It has taken me a long time to understand myself. I still have a lot further to go with discovery; however, one of the most important things I have learned is to not worry what others think of me. Their opinions are not my psyche dilemma, but theirs. My opinion is my only concern, and I don't share it unless asked.

It matters only to me what I think of myself and how I treat everything in life. If I'd cared what people thought of me, I would never have come out or done any of the things I have done. I love who I have become, on my own.

My message for you is simple: Be your strong true self at all costs. You are the only person you ever have to answer to—no one else. This is a proven fact, as I have had people come into their own with acceptance based on what I have done, showing pride in myself, being in the military or not. These folks are now working their own brand of magic in their lives. There are few things better than affecting others in a way that changes their lives so that they hear their own voice calling—and being heard. I'm proud of this.

My life will always have struggles and strife—that's what life is all about—but I know who I am. I know my limitations, and my boundaries are firm. I look forward to challenges as they arise, and I grow with them. My challenge is to learn from my surroundings and what I experience in this amazing journey we call life.

As an empath, I see people and feel their energy. I either stay to engage or turn away. I gained "me" because of everything I've been through and the acute nature of my instincts that keep me aware. Nothing much gets by my intuition. My own self-awareness and confidence are firm; however, my confidence levels continue to be tested and honed with each new adventure I encounter.

All I ever wanted was to be happy and loved. I never felt it growing up, but I feel it now. I've created both for myself and I'm at peace. My contract, which I became aware of through my personal development courses, is this: I am a strong, kind, loving, sexy man. The world is a beautiful place to explore. That's where I'll be. I am definitely not where I was.

Much love and gratitude,

Steve

Steve, happy to be alive, 2022.

Afterword

Reading my words describing my life and all I went through to maintain who I am—not just surviving but thriving—makes me sit back in disbelief. I remember these situations and many others not mentioned in this book with detailed emotions and feelings attached. I find myself being grateful for recognizing my own power and desire to make a difference, even when I didn't have either of those as strongholds in my early psyche. I am most proud of who I am at this point in my life, of my friendships, accomplishments, and above all, my heart.

I recently learned that my brother, the one next to me in age, told a few friends of mine that I have the biggest heart of all of them put together. He said that if a normal size heart is this big, Steven's is three times that size. He has since told me that he admires me and how I am living my life. He made me feel he loves me. This was the first time in my life he said things like this to me. Time does change things and people.

I also want to extend one last note of appreciation: "Thank you, Dad. I'm proud to be your son and carry your wonderful heart. Even though you didn't live long enough to see who I would eventually become, you can rest assured, I carried on and the world knows my big heart came from you."

Thank you for reading my book. The Universe has connected us in ways we may never know. I do know I wrote this to help you recognize your own power and worth. Stay strong and be selective with the alignment of your thoughts, choices, and relationships. Everything has consequences, both good and bad. So be careful, realize who you are, and when you are ready, let the world know the beautiful power of being you.

About the Author

Steve Zeiger was the eldest child born into a farming family. Raised in a rural farming community, his family and school experiences compelled him to honor his unique qualities, which did not include farming. Determined to seek out new cultures and experiences, he joined the Air Force after he graduated from high school. From basic training in January 1981 to his retirement in 2007, the Air force recognized his integrity, can-do attitude, and resilience. In 2012, he started volunteering and became an advocate for LGBTQIA+ service men and women. Steve's commitment resulted in many firsts, including the addition of the Military Walking in the annual Pride Parade in St. Louis, a Wreath Laying Ceremony at the Soldiers Memorial, and the lighting of the Memorial in rainbow colors. Steve continues to follow his adventurous spirit and has made a career out of seasonal work. In all that he is and does, the natural world remains his sanctuary.

Made in the USA
Monee, IL
01 July 2023